C-742   CAREER EXAMINATION SERIES

This is your
PASSBOOK for...

Signal Maintainer

Test Preparation Study Guide
Questions & Answers

COPYRIGHT NOTICE

This book is SOLELY intended for, is sold ONLY to, and its use is RESTRICTED to individual, bona fide applicants or candidates who qualify by virtue of having seriously filed applications for appropriate license, certificate, professional and/or promotional advancement, higher school matriculation, scholarship, or other legitimate requirements of education and/or governmental authorities.

This book is NOT intended for use, class instruction, tutoring, training, duplication, copying, reprinting, excerption, or adaptation, etc., by:

1) Other publishers
2) Proprietors and/or Instructors of "Coaching" and/or Preparatory Courses
3) Personnel and/or Training Divisions of commercial, industrial, and governmental organizations
4) Schools, colleges, or universities and/or their departments and staffs, including teachers and other personnel
5) Testing Agencies or Bureaus
6) Study groups which seek by the purchase of a single volume to copy and/or duplicate and/or adapt this material for use by the group as a whole without having purchased individual volumes for each of the members of the group
7) Et al.

Such persons would be in violation of appropriate Federal and State statutes.

PROVISION OF LICENSING AGREEMENTS – Recognized educational, commercial, industrial, and governmental institutions and organizations, and others legitimately engaged in educational pursuits, including training, testing, and measurement activities, may address request for a licensing agreement to the copyright owners, who will determine whether, and under what conditions, including fees and charges, the materials in this book may be used them. In other words, a licensing facility exists for the legitimate use of the material in this book on other than an individual basis. However, it is asseverated and affirmed here that the material in this book CANNOT be used without the receipt of the express permission of such a licensing agreement from the Publishers. Inquiries re licensing should be addressed to the company, attention rights and permissions department.

All rights reserved, including the right of reproduction in whole or in part, in any form or by any means, electronic or mechanical, including photocopying, recording, or by any information storage and retrieval system, without permission in writing from the Publisher.

Copyright © 2025 by

National Learning Corporation

212 Michael Drive, Syosset, NY 11791
(516) 921-8888 • www.passbooks.com
E-mail: info@passbooks.com

PASSBOOK® SERIES

THE *PASSBOOK® SERIES* has been created to prepare applicants and candidates for the ultimate academic battlefield – the examination room.

At some time in our lives, each and every one of us may be required to take an examination – for validation, matriculation, admission, qualification, registration, certification, or licensure.

Based on the assumption that every applicant or candidate has met the basic formal educational standards, has taken the required number of courses, and read the necessary texts, the *PASSBOOK® SERIES* furnishes the one special preparation which may assure passing with confidence, instead of failing with insecurity. Examination questions – together with answers – are furnished as the basic vehicle for study so that the mysteries of the examination and its compounding difficulties may be eliminated or diminished by a sure method.

This book is meant to help you pass your examination provided that you qualify and are serious in your objective.

The entire field is reviewed through the huge store of content information which is succinctly presented through a provocative and challenging approach – the question-and-answer method.

A climate of success is established by furnishing the correct answers at the end of each test.

You soon learn to recognize types of questions, forms of questions, and patterns of questioning. You may even begin to anticipate expected outcomes.

You perceive that many questions are repeated or adapted so that you can gain acute insights, which may enable you to score many sure points.

You learn how to confront new questions, or types of questions, and to attack them confidently and work out the correct answers.

You note objectives and emphases, and recognize pitfalls and dangers, so that you may make positive educational adjustments.

Moreover, you are kept fully informed in relation to new concepts, methods, practices, and directions in the field.

You discover that you are actually taking the examination all the time: you are preparing for the examination by "taking" an examination, not by reading extraneous and/or supererogatory textbooks.

In short, this PASSBOOK®, used directedly, should be an important factor in helping you to pass your test.

SIGNAL MAINTAINER

DUTIES AND RESPONSIBILITIES

To maintain, install, inspect, test, alter and repair the railroad signal system on the road and in the shop, including: all-electric, electro-pneumatic, and relay, and mechanical interlocking machines, centralized traffic control machines, switch machines, automatic train stops, color light and semaphore signals, and associated power and control equipment; if assigned, perform inspection work on new equipment and material at manufacturing plants; keep records; perform such other duties as the transit authority is authorized by law to prescribe in its regulations.

SCOPE OF THE EXAMINATION

The test will include questions and tasks relating to the installation, testing, maintenance and repair of electrical, electronic and electro-mechanical systems, including the selection and use of appropriate tools, materials and measuring devices; electrical theory and principles; related mechanical work; reading and interpreting technical drawings; shop math; safe work practices and procedures; and questions designed to determine the candidate's relative judgment and knowledge with respect to the principles involved in signal circuits and the ability to read and interpret signal circuit drawings, maintenance procedures and inspection methods, signal equipment, proper relationships with other transit authority personnel, safety procedures, Transit Authority rules and procedures, troubleshooting procedures on signals, basic electrical principles, and other related areas pertaining to the maintenance and inspection of the railroad signal system.

HOW TO TAKE A TEST

I. YOU MUST PASS AN EXAMINATION

A. *WHAT EVERY CANDIDATE SHOULD KNOW*

Examination applicants often ask us for help in preparing for the written test. What can I study in advance? What kinds of questions will be asked? How will the test be given? How will the papers be graded?

As an applicant for a civil service examination, you may be wondering about some of these things. Our purpose here is to suggest effective methods of advance study and to describe civil service examinations.

Your chances for success on this examination can be increased if you know how to prepare. Those "pre-examination jitters" can be reduced if you know what to expect. You can even experience an adventure in good citizenship if you know why civil service exams are given.

B. *WHY ARE CIVIL SERVICE EXAMINATIONS GIVEN?*

Civil service examinations are important to you in two ways. As a citizen, you want public jobs filled by employees who know how to do their work. As a job seeker, you want a fair chance to compete for that job on an equal footing with other candidates. The best-known means of accomplishing this two-fold goal is the competitive examination.

Exams are widely publicized throughout the nation. They may be administered for jobs in federal, state, city, municipal, town or village governments or agencies.

Any citizen may apply, with some limitations, such as the age or residence of applicants. Your experience and education may be reviewed to see whether you meet the requirements for the particular examination. When these requirements exist, they are reasonable and applied consistently to all applicants. Thus, a competitive examination may cause you some uneasiness now, but it is your privilege and safeguard.

C. *HOW ARE CIVIL SERVICE EXAMS DEVELOPED?*

Examinations are carefully written by trained technicians who are specialists in the field known as "psychological measurement," in consultation with recognized authorities in the field of work that the test will cover. These experts recommend the subject matter areas or skills to be tested; only those knowledges or skills important to your success on the job are included. The most reliable books and source materials available are used as references. Together, the experts and technicians judge the difficulty level of the questions.

Test technicians know how to phrase questions so that the problem is clearly stated. Their ethics do not permit "trick" or "catch" questions. Questions may have been tried out on sample groups, or subjected to statistical analysis, to determine their usefulness.

Written tests are often used in combination with performance tests, ratings of training and experience, and oral interviews. All of these measures combine to form the best-known means of finding the right person for the right job.

II. HOW TO PASS THE WRITTEN TEST

A. NATURE OF THE EXAMINATION

To prepare intelligently for civil service examinations, you should know how they differ from school examinations you have taken. In school you were assigned certain definite pages to read or subjects to cover. The examination questions were quite detailed and usually emphasized memory. Civil service exams, on the other hand, try to discover your present ability to perform the duties of a position, plus your potentiality to learn these duties. In other words, a civil service exam attempts to predict how successful you will be. Questions cover such a broad area that they cannot be as minute and detailed as school exam questions.

In the public service similar kinds of work, or positions, are grouped together in one "class." This process is known as *position-classification*. All the positions in a class are paid according to the salary range for that class. One class title covers all of these positions, and they are all tested by the same examination.

B. FOUR BASIC STEPS

1) Study the announcement

How, then, can you know what subjects to study? Our best answer is: "Learn as much as possible about the class of positions for which you've applied." The exam will test the knowledge, skills and abilities needed to do the work.

Your most valuable source of information about the position you want is the official exam announcement. This announcement lists the training and experience qualifications. Check these standards and apply only if you come reasonably close to meeting them.

The brief description of the position in the examination announcement offers some clues to the subjects which will be tested. Think about the job itself. Review the duties in your mind. Can you perform them, or are there some in which you are rusty? Fill in the blank spots in your preparation.

Many jurisdictions preview the written test in the exam announcement by including a section called "Knowledge and Abilities Required," "Scope of the Examination," or some similar heading. Here you will find out specifically what fields will be tested.

2) Review your own background

Once you learn in general what the position is all about, and what you need to know to do the work, ask yourself which subjects you already know fairly well and which need improvement. You may wonder whether to concentrate on improving your strong areas or on building some background in your fields of weakness. When the announcement has specified "some knowledge" or "considerable knowledge," or has used adjectives like "beginning principles of..." or "advanced ... methods," you can get a clue as to the number and difficulty of questions to be asked in any given field. More questions, and hence broader coverage, would be included for those subjects which are more important in the work. Now weigh your strengths and weaknesses against the job requirements and prepare accordingly.

3) Determine the level of the position

Another way to tell how intensively you should prepare is to understand the level of the job for which you are applying. Is it the entering level? In other words, is this the position in which beginners in a field of work are hired? Or is it an intermediate or advanced level? Sometimes this is indicated by such words as "Junior" or "Senior" in the class title. Other jurisdictions use Roman numerals to designate the level – Clerk I, Clerk II, for example. The word "Supervisor" sometimes appears in the title. If the level is not indicated by the title, check the description of duties. Will you be working under very close supervision, or will you have responsibility for independent decisions in this work?

4) Choose appropriate study materials

Now that you know the subjects to be examined and the relative amount of each subject to be covered, you can choose suitable study materials. For beginning level jobs, or even advanced ones, if you have a pronounced weakness in some aspect of your training, read a modern, standard textbook in that field. Be sure it is up to date and has general coverage. Such books are normally available at your library, and the librarian will be glad to help you locate one. For entry-level positions, questions of appropriate difficulty are chosen – neither highly advanced questions, nor those too simple. Such questions require careful thought but not advanced training.

If the position for which you are applying is technical or advanced, you will read more advanced, specialized material. If you are already familiar with the basic principles of your field, elementary textbooks would waste your time. Concentrate on advanced textbooks and technical periodicals. Think through the concepts and review difficult problems in your field.

These are all general sources. You can get more ideas on your own initiative, following these leads. For example, training manuals and publications of the government agency which employs workers in your field can be useful, particularly for technical and professional positions. A letter or visit to the government department involved may result in more specific study suggestions, and certainly will provide you with a more definite idea of the exact nature of the position you are seeking.

III. KINDS OF TESTS

Tests are used for purposes other than measuring knowledge and ability to perform specified duties. For some positions, it is equally important to test ability to make adjustments to new situations or to profit from training. In others, basic mental abilities not dependent on information are essential. Questions which test these things may not appear as pertinent to the duties of the position as those which test for knowledge and information. Yet they are often highly important parts of a fair examination. For very general questions, it is almost impossible to help you direct your study efforts. What we can do is to point out some of the more common of these general abilities needed in public service positions and describe some typical questions.

1) General information

Broad, general information has been found useful for predicting job success in some kinds of work. This is tested in a variety of ways, from vocabulary lists to questions about current events. Basic background in some field of work, such as sociology or economics, may be sampled in a group of questions. Often these are principles which have become familiar to most persons through exposure rather than through formal training. It is difficult to advise you how to study for these questions; being alert to the world around you is our best suggestion.

2) Verbal ability

An example of an ability needed in many positions is verbal or language ability. Verbal ability is, in brief, the ability to use and understand words. Vocabulary and grammar tests are typical measures of this ability. Reading comprehension or paragraph interpretation questions are common in many kinds of civil service tests. You are given a paragraph of written material and asked to find its central meaning.

3) Numerical ability

Number skills can be tested by the familiar arithmetic problem, by checking paired lists of numbers to see which are alike and which are different, or by interpreting charts and graphs. In the latter test, a graph may be printed in the test booklet which you are asked to use as the basis for answering questions.

4) Observation

A popular test for law-enforcement positions is the observation test. A picture is shown to you for several minutes, then taken away. Questions about the picture test your ability to observe both details and larger elements.

5) Following directions

In many positions in the public service, the employee must be able to carry out written instructions dependably and accurately. You may be given a chart with several columns, each column listing a variety of information. The questions require you to carry out directions involving the information given in the chart.

6) Skills and aptitudes

Performance tests effectively measure some manual skills and aptitudes. When the skill is one in which you are trained, such as typing or shorthand, you can practice. These tests are often very much like those given in business school or high school courses. For many of the other skills and aptitudes, however, no short-time preparation can be made. Skills and abilities natural to you or that you have developed throughout your lifetime are being tested.

Many of the general questions just described provide all the data needed to answer the questions and ask you to use your reasoning ability to find the answers. Your best preparation for these tests, as well as for tests of facts and ideas, is to be at your physical and mental best. You, no doubt, have your own methods of getting into an exam-taking mood and keeping "in shape." The next section lists some ideas on this subject.

IV. KINDS OF QUESTIONS

Only rarely is the "essay" question, which you answer in narrative form, used in civil service tests. Civil service tests are usually of the short-answer type. Full instructions for answering these questions will be given to you at the examination. But in case this is your first experience with short-answer questions and separate answer sheets, here is what you need to know:

1) Multiple-choice Questions

Most popular of the short-answer questions is the "multiple choice" or "best answer" question. It can be used, for example, to test for factual knowledge, ability to solve problems or judgment in meeting situations found at work.

A multiple-choice question is normally one of three types—
- It can begin with an incomplete statement followed by several possible endings. You are to find the one ending which *best* completes the statement, although some of the others may not be entirely wrong.
- It can also be a complete statement in the form of a question which is answered by choosing one of the statements listed.

- It can be in the form of a problem – again you select the best answer.

Here is an example of a multiple-choice question with a discussion which should give you some clues as to the method for choosing the right answer:

When an employee has a complaint about his assignment, the action which will *best* help him overcome his difficulty is to
  A. discuss his difficulty with his coworkers
  B. take the problem to the head of the organization
  C. take the problem to the person who gave him the assignment
  D. say nothing to anyone about his complaint

In answering this question, you should study each of the choices to find which is best. Consider choice "A" – Certainly an employee may discuss his complaint with fellow employees, but no change or improvement can result, and the complaint remains unresolved. Choice "B" is a poor choice since the head of the organization probably does not know what assignment you have been given, and taking your problem to him is known as "going over the head" of the supervisor. The supervisor, or person who made the assignment, is the person who can clarify it or correct any injustice. Choice "C" is, therefore, correct. To say nothing, as in choice "D," is unwise. Supervisors have and interest in knowing the problems employees are facing, and the employee is seeking a solution to his problem.

2) True/False Questions

The "true/false" or "right/wrong" form of question is sometimes used. Here a complete statement is given. Your job is to decide whether the statement is right or wrong.

SAMPLE: A roaming cell-phone call to a nearby city costs less than a non-roaming call to a distant city.

This statement is wrong, or false, since roaming calls are more expensive.
This is not a complete list of all possible question forms, although most of the others are variations of these common types. You will always get complete directions for answering questions. Be sure you understand *how* to mark your answers – ask questions until you do.

V. RECORDING YOUR ANSWERS

Computer terminals are used more and more today for many different kinds of exams.
For an examination with very few applicants, you may be told to record your answers in the test booklet itself. Separate answer sheets are much more common. If this separate answer sheet is to be scored by machine – and this is often the case – it is highly important that you mark your answers correctly in order to get credit.
An electronic scoring machine is often used in civil service offices because of the speed with which papers can be scored. Machine-scored answer sheets must be marked with a pencil, which will be given to you. This pencil has a high graphite content which responds to the electronic scoring machine. As a matter of fact, stray dots may register as answers, so do not let your pencil rest on the answer sheet while you are pondering the correct answer. Also, if your pencil lead breaks or is otherwise defective, ask for another.

Since the answer sheet will be dropped in a slot in the scoring machine, be careful not to bend the corners or get the paper crumpled.

The answer sheet normally has five vertical columns of numbers, with 30 numbers to a column. These numbers correspond to the question numbers in your test booklet. After each number, going across the page are four or five pairs of dotted lines. These short dotted lines have small letters or numbers above them. The first two pairs may also have a "T" or "F" above the letters. This indicates that the first two pairs only are to be used if the questions are of the true-false type. If the questions are multiple choice, disregard the "T" and "F" and pay attention only to the small letters or numbers.

Answer your questions in the manner of the sample that follows:

32. The largest city in the United States is
    A. Washington, D.C.
    B. New York City
    C. Chicago
    D. Detroit
    E. San Francisco

1) Choose the answer you think is best. (New York City is the largest, so "B" is correct.)
2) Find the row of dotted lines numbered the same as the question you are answering. (Find row number 32)
3) Find the pair of dotted lines corresponding to the answer. (Find the pair of lines under the mark "B.")
4) Make a solid black mark between the dotted lines.

VI. BEFORE THE TEST

Common sense will help you find procedures to follow to get ready for an examination. Too many of us, however, overlook these sensible measures. Indeed, nervousness and fatigue have been found to be the most serious reasons why applicants fail to do their best on civil service tests. Here is a list of reminders:

- Begin your preparation early – Don't wait until the last minute to go scurrying around for books and materials or to find out what the position is all about.
- Prepare continuously – An hour a night for a week is better than an all-night cram session. This has been definitely established. What is more, a night a week for a month will return better dividends than crowding your study into a shorter period of time.
- Locate the place of the exam – You have been sent a notice telling you when and where to report for the examination. If the location is in a different town or otherwise unfamiliar to you, it would be well to inquire the best route and learn something about the building.
- Relax the night before the test – Allow your mind to rest. Do not study at all that night. Plan some mild recreation or diversion; then go to bed early and get a good night's sleep.
- Get up early enough to make a leisurely trip to the place for the test – This way unforeseen events, traffic snarls, unfamiliar buildings, etc. will not upset you.
- Dress comfortably – A written test is not a fashion show. You will be known by number and not by name, so wear something comfortable.

- Leave excess paraphernalia at home – Shopping bags and odd bundles will get in your way. You need bring only the items mentioned in the official notice you received; usually everything you need is provided. Do not bring reference books to the exam. They will only confuse those last minutes and be taken away from you when in the test room.
- Arrive somewhat ahead of time – If because of transportation schedules you must get there very early, bring a newspaper or magazine to take your mind off yourself while waiting.
- Locate the examination room – When you have found the proper room, you will be directed to the seat or part of the room where you will sit. Sometimes you are given a sheet of instructions to read while you are waiting. Do not fill out any forms until you are told to do so; just read them and be prepared.
- Relax and prepare to listen to the instructions
- If you have any physical problem that may keep you from doing your best, be sure to tell the test administrator. If you are sick or in poor health, you really cannot do your best on the exam. You can come back and take the test some other time.

VII. AT THE TEST

The day of the test is here and you have the test booklet in your hand. The temptation to get going is very strong. Caution! There is more to success than knowing the right answers. You must know how to identify your papers and understand variations in the type of short-answer question used in this particular examination. Follow these suggestions for maximum results from your efforts:

1) Cooperate with the monitor

The test administrator has a duty to create a situation in which you can be as much at ease as possible. He will give instructions, tell you when to begin, check to see that you are marking your answer sheet correctly, and so on. He is not there to guard you, although he will see that your competitors do not take unfair advantage. He wants to help you do your best.

2) Listen to all instructions

Don't jump the gun! Wait until you understand all directions. In most civil service tests you get more time than you need to answer the questions. So don't be in a hurry. Read each word of instructions until you clearly understand the meaning. Study the examples, listen to all announcements and follow directions. Ask questions if you do not understand what to do.

3) Identify your papers

Civil service exams are usually identified by number only. You will be assigned a number; you must not put your name on your test papers. Be sure to copy your number correctly. Since more than one exam may be given, copy your exact examination title.

4) Plan your time

Unless you are told that a test is a "speed" or "rate of work" test, speed itself is usually not important. Time enough to answer all the questions will be provided, but this does not mean that you have all day. An overall time limit has been set. Divide the total time (in minutes) by the number of questions to determine the approximate time you have for each question.

5) Do not linger over difficult questions

If you come across a difficult question, mark it with a paper clip (useful to have along) and come back to it when you have been through the booklet. One caution if you do this – be sure to skip a number on your answer sheet as well. Check often to be sure that you have not lost your place and that you are marking in the row numbered the same as the question you are answering.

6) Read the questions

Be sure you know what the question asks! Many capable people are unsuccessful because they failed to *read* the questions correctly.

7) Answer all questions

Unless you have been instructed that a penalty will be deducted for incorrect answers, it is better to guess than to omit a question.

8) Speed tests

It is often better NOT to guess on speed tests. It has been found that on timed tests people are tempted to spend the last few seconds before time is called in marking answers at random – without even reading them – in the hope of picking up a few extra points. To discourage this practice, the instructions may warn you that your score will be "corrected" for guessing. That is, a penalty will be applied. The incorrect answers will be deducted from the correct ones, or some other penalty formula will be used.

9) Review your answers

If you finish before time is called, go back to the questions you guessed or omitted to give them further thought. Review other answers if you have time.

10) Return your test materials

If you are ready to leave before others have finished or time is called, take ALL your materials to the monitor and leave quietly. Never take any test material with you. The monitor can discover whose papers are not complete, and taking a test booklet may be grounds for disqualification.

VIII. EXAMINATION TECHNIQUES

1) Read the general instructions carefully. These are usually printed on the first page of the exam booklet. As a rule, these instructions refer to the timing of the examination; the fact that you should not start work until the signal and must stop work at a signal, etc. If there are any *special* instructions, such as a choice of questions to be answered, make sure that you note this instruction carefully.

2) When you are ready to start work on the examination, that is as soon as the signal has been given, read the instructions to each question booklet, underline any key words or phrases, such as *least, best, outline, describe* and the like. In this way you will tend to answer as requested rather than discover on reviewing your paper that you *listed without describing*, that you selected the *worst* choice rather than the *best* choice, etc.

3) If the examination is of the objective or multiple-choice type – that is, each question will also give a series of possible answers: A, B, C or D, and you are called upon to select the best answer and write the letter next to that answer on your answer paper – it is advisable to start answering each question in turn. There may be anywhere from 50 to 100 such questions in the three or four hours allotted and you can see how much time would be taken if you read through all the questions before beginning to answer any. Furthermore, if you come across a question or group of questions which you know would be difficult to answer, it would undoubtedly affect your handling of all the other questions.

4) If the examination is of the essay type and contains but a few questions, it is a moot point as to whether you should read all the questions before starting to answer any one. Of course, if you are given a choice – say five out of seven and the like – then it is essential to read all the questions so you can eliminate the two that are most difficult. If, however, you are asked to answer all the questions, there may be danger in trying to answer the easiest one first because you may find that you will spend too much time on it. The best technique is to answer the first question, then proceed to the second, etc.

5) Time your answers. Before the exam begins, write down the time it started, then add the time allowed for the examination and write down the time it must be completed, then divide the time available somewhat as follows:
   - If 3-1/2 hours are allowed, that would be 210 minutes. If you have 80 objective-type questions, that would be an average of 2-1/2 minutes per question. Allow yourself no more than 2 minutes per question, or a total of 160 minutes, which will permit about 50 minutes to review.
   - If for the time allotment of 210 minutes there are 7 essay questions to answer, that would average about 30 minutes a question. Give yourself only 25 minutes per question so that you have about 35 minutes to review.

6) The most important instruction is to *read each question* and make sure you know what is wanted. The second most important instruction is to *time yourself properly* so that you answer every question. The third most important instruction is to *answer every question*. Guess if you have to but include something for each question. Remember that you will receive no credit for a blank and will probably receive some credit if you write something in answer to an essay question. If you guess a letter – say "B" for a multiple-choice question – you may have guessed right. If you leave a blank as an answer to a multiple-choice question, the examiners may respect your feelings but it will not add a point to your score. Some exams may penalize you for wrong answers, so in such cases *only*, you may not want to guess unless you have some basis for your answer.

7) Suggestions
   a. Objective-type questions
      1. Examine the question booklet for proper sequence of pages and questions
      2. Read all instructions carefully
      3. Skip any question which seems too difficult; return to it after all other questions have been answered
      4. Apportion your time properly; do not spend too much time on any single question or group of questions

5. Note and underline key words – *all, most, fewest, least, best, worst, same, opposite,* etc.
6. Pay particular attention to negatives
7. Note unusual option, e.g., unduly long, short, complex, different or similar in content to the body of the question
8. Observe the use of "hedging" words – *probably, may, most likely,* etc.
9. Make sure that your answer is put next to the same number as the question
10. Do not second-guess unless you have good reason to believe the second answer is definitely more correct
11. Cross out original answer if you decide another answer is more accurate; do not erase until you are ready to hand your paper in
12. Answer all questions; guess unless instructed otherwise
13. Leave time for review

b. Essay questions
1. Read each question carefully
2. Determine exactly what is wanted. Underline key words or phrases.
3. Decide on outline or paragraph answer
4. Include many different points and elements unless asked to develop any one or two points or elements
5. Show impartiality by giving pros and cons unless directed to select one side only
6. Make and write down any assumptions you find necessary to answer the questions
7. Watch your English, grammar, punctuation and choice of words
8. Time your answers; don't crowd material

8) Answering the essay question

Most essay questions can be answered by framing the specific response around several key words or ideas. Here are a few such key words or ideas:

M's: manpower, materials, methods, money, management
P's: purpose, program, policy, plan, procedure, practice, problems, pitfalls, personnel, public relations

  a. Six basic steps in handling problems:
    1. Preliminary plan and background development
    2. Collect information, data and facts
    3. Analyze and interpret information, data and facts
    4. Analyze and develop solutions as well as make recommendations
    5. Prepare report and sell recommendations
    6. Install recommendations and follow up effectiveness

  b. Pitfalls to avoid
    1. *Taking things for granted* – A statement of the situation does not necessarily imply that each of the elements is necessarily true; for example, a complaint may be invalid and biased so that all that can be taken for granted is that a complaint has been registered

2. *Considering only one side of a situation* – Wherever possible, indicate several alternatives and then point out the reasons you selected the best one
3. *Failing to indicate follow up* – Whenever your answer indicates action on your part, make certain that you will take proper follow-up action to see how successful your recommendations, procedures or actions turn out to be
4. *Taking too long in answering any single question* – Remember to time your answers properly

IX. AFTER THE TEST

Scoring procedures differ in detail among civil service jurisdictions although the general principles are the same. Whether the papers are hand-scored or graded by machine we have described, they are nearly always graded by number. That is, the person who marks the paper knows only the number – never the name – of the applicant. Not until all the papers have been graded will they be matched with names. If other tests, such as training and experience or oral interview ratings have been given, scores will be combined. Different parts of the examination usually have different weights. For example, the written test might count 60 percent of the final grade, and a rating of training and experience 40 percent. In many jurisdictions, veterans will have a certain number of points added to their grades.

After the final grade has been determined, the names are placed in grade order and an eligible list is established. There are various methods for resolving ties between those who get the same final grade – probably the most common is to place first the name of the person whose application was received first. Job offers are made from the eligible list in the order the names appear on it. You will be notified of your grade and your rank as soon as all these computations have been made. This will be done as rapidly as possible.

People who are found to meet the requirements in the announcement are called "eligibles." Their names are put on a list of eligible candidates. An eligible's chances of getting a job depend on how high he stands on this list and how fast agencies are filling jobs from the list.

When a job is to be filled from a list of eligibles, the agency asks for the names of people on the list of eligibles for that job. When the civil service commission receives this request, it sends to the agency the names of the three people highest on this list. Or, if the job to be filled has specialized requirements, the office sends the agency the names of the top three persons who meet these requirements from the general list.

The appointing officer makes a choice from among the three people whose names were sent to him. If the selected person accepts the appointment, the names of the others are put back on the list to be considered for future openings.

That is the rule in hiring from all kinds of eligible lists, whether they are for typist, carpenter, chemist, or something else. For every vacancy, the appointing officer has his choice of any one of the top three eligibles on the list. This explains why the person whose name is on top of the list sometimes does not get an appointment when some of the persons lower on the list do. If the appointing officer chooses the second or third eligible, the No. 1 eligible does not get a job at once, but stays on the list until he is appointed or the list is terminated.

X. HOW TO PASS THE INTERVIEW TEST

The examination for which you applied requires an oral interview test. You have already taken the written test and you are now being called for the interview test – the final part of the formal examination.

You may think that it is not possible to prepare for an interview test and that there are no procedures to follow during an interview. Our purpose is to point out some things you can do in advance that will help you and some good rules to follow and pitfalls to avoid while you are being interviewed.

What is an interview supposed to test?

The written examination is designed to test the technical knowledge and competence of the candidate; the oral is designed to evaluate intangible qualities, not readily measured otherwise, and to establish a list showing the relative fitness of each candidate – as measured against his competitors – for the position sought. Scoring is not on the basis of "right" and "wrong," but on a sliding scale of values ranging from "not passable" to "outstanding." As a matter of fact, it is possible to achieve a relatively low score without a single "incorrect" answer because of evident weakness in the qualities being measured.

Occasionally, an examination may consist entirely of an oral test – either an individual or a group oral. In such cases, information is sought concerning the technical knowledges and abilities of the candidate, since there has been no written examination for this purpose. More commonly, however, an oral test is used to supplement a written examination.

Who conducts interviews?

The composition of oral boards varies among different jurisdictions. In nearly all, a representative of the personnel department serves as chairman. One of the members of the board may be a representative of the department in which the candidate would work. In some cases, "outside experts" are used, and, frequently, a businessman or some other representative of the general public is asked to serve. Labor and management or other special groups may be represented. The aim is to secure the services of experts in the appropriate field.

However the board is composed, it is a good idea (and not at all improper or unethical) to ascertain in advance of the interview who the members are and what groups they represent. When you are introduced to them, you will have some idea of their backgrounds and interests, and at least you will not stutter and stammer over their names.

What should be done before the interview?

While knowledge about the board members is useful and takes some of the surprise element out of the interview, there is other preparation which is more substantive. It *is* possible to prepare for an oral interview – in several ways:

1) Keep a copy of your application and review it carefully before the interview

This may be the only document before the oral board, and the starting point of the interview. Know what education and experience you have listed there, and the sequence and dates of all of it. Sometimes the board will ask you to review the highlights of your experience for them; you should not have to hem and haw doing it.

2) Study the class specification and the examination announcement

Usually, the oral board has one or both of these to guide them. The qualities, characteristics or knowledges required by the position sought are stated in these documents. They offer valuable clues as to the nature of the oral interview. For example, if the job involves supervisory responsibilities, the announcement will usually indicate that knowledge of modern supervisory methods and the qualifications of the candidate as a supervisor will be tested. If so, you can expect such questions, frequently in the form of a hypothetical situation which you are expected to solve. NEVER go into an oral without knowledge of the duties and responsibilities of the job you seek.

3) Think through each qualification required

Try to visualize the kind of questions you would ask if you were a board member. How well could you answer them? Try especially to appraise your own knowledge and background in each area, *measured against the job sought*, and identify any areas in which you are weak. Be critical and realistic – do not flatter yourself.

4) Do some general reading in areas in which you feel you may be weak

For example, if the job involves supervision and your past experience has NOT, some general reading in supervisory methods and practices, particularly in the field of human relations, might be useful. Do NOT study agency procedures or detailed manuals. The oral board will be testing your understanding and capacity, not your memory.

5) Get a good night's sleep and watch your general health and mental attitude

You will want a clear head at the interview. Take care of a cold or any other minor ailment, and of course, no hangovers.

What should be done on the day of the interview?

Now comes the day of the interview itself. Give yourself plenty of time to get there. Plan to arrive somewhat ahead of the scheduled time, particularly if your appointment is in the fore part of the day. If a previous candidate fails to appear, the board might be ready for you a bit early. By early afternoon an oral board is almost invariably behind schedule if there are many candidates, and you may have to wait. Take along a book or magazine to read, or your application to review, but leave any extraneous material in the waiting room when you go in for your interview. In any event, relax and compose yourself.

The matter of dress is important. The board is forming impressions about you – from your experience, your manners, your attitude, and your appearance. Give your personal appearance careful attention. Dress your best, but not your flashiest. Choose conservative, appropriate clothing, and be sure it is immaculate. This is a business interview, and your appearance should indicate that you regard it as such. Besides, being well groomed and properly dressed will help boost your confidence.

Sooner or later, someone will call your name and escort you into the interview room. *This is it.* From here on you are on your own. It is too late for any more preparation. But remember, you asked for this opportunity to prove your fitness, and you are here because your request was granted.

What happens when you go in?

The usual sequence of events will be as follows: The clerk (who is often the board stenographer) will introduce you to the chairman of the oral board, who will introduce you to the other members of the board. Acknowledge the introductions before you sit down. Do not be surprised if you find a microphone facing you or a stenotypist sitting by. Oral interviews are usually recorded in the event of an appeal or other review.

Usually the chairman of the board will open the interview by reviewing the highlights of your education and work experience from your application – primarily for the benefit of the other members of the board, as well as to get the material into the record. Do not interrupt or comment unless there is an error or significant misinterpretation; if that is the case, do not hesitate. But do not quibble about insignificant matters. Also, he will usually ask you some question about your education, experience or your present job – partly to get you to start talking and to establish the interviewing "rapport." He may start the actual questioning, or turn it over to one of the other members. Frequently, each member undertakes the questioning on a particular area, one in which he is perhaps most competent, so you can expect each member to participate in the examination. Because time is limited, you may also expect some rather abrupt switches in the direction the questioning takes, so do not be upset by it. Normally, a board member will not pursue a single line of questioning unless he discovers a particular strength or weakness.

After each member has participated, the chairman will usually ask whether any member has any further questions, then will ask you if you have anything you wish to add. Unless you are expecting this question, it may floor you. Worse, it may start you off on an extended, extemporaneous speech. The board is not usually seeking more information. The question is principally to offer you a last opportunity to present further qualifications or to indicate that you have nothing to add. So, if you feel that a significant qualification or characteristic has been overlooked, it is proper to point it out in a sentence or so. Do not compliment the board on the thoroughness of their examination – they have been sketchy, and you know it. If you wish, merely say, "No thank you, I have nothing further to add." This is a point where you can "talk yourself out" of a good impression or fail to present an important bit of information. Remember, *you close the interview yourself.*

The chairman will then say, "That is all, Mr. _____, thank you." Do not be startled; the interview is over, and quicker than you think. Thank him, gather your belongings and take your leave. Save your sigh of relief for the other side of the door.

How to put your best foot forward

Throughout this entire process, you may feel that the board individually and collectively is trying to pierce your defenses, seek out your hidden weaknesses and embarrass and confuse you. Actually, this is not true. They are obliged to make an appraisal of your qualifications for the job you are seeking, and they want to see you in your best light. Remember, they must interview all candidates and a non-cooperative candidate may become a failure in spite of their best efforts to bring out his qualifications. Here are 15 suggestions that will help you:

1) Be natural – Keep your attitude confident, not cocky

If you are not confident that you can do the job, do not expect the board to be. Do not apologize for your weaknesses, try to bring out your strong points. The board is interested in a positive, not negative, presentation. Cockiness will antagonize any board member and make him wonder if you are covering up a weakness by a false show of strength.

2) Get comfortable, but don't lounge or sprawl

Sit erectly but not stiffly. A careless posture may lead the board to conclude that you are careless in other things, or at least that you are not impressed by the importance of the occasion. Either conclusion is natural, even if incorrect. Do not fuss with your clothing, a pencil or an ashtray. Your hands may occasionally be useful to emphasize a point; do not let them become a point of distraction.

3) Do not wisecrack or make small talk

This is a serious situation, and your attitude should show that you consider it as such. Further, the time of the board is limited – they do not want to waste it, and neither should you.

4) Do not exaggerate your experience or abilities
In the first place, from information in the application or other interviews and sources, the board may know more about you than you think. Secondly, you probably will not get away with it. An experienced board is rather adept at spotting such a situation, so do not take the chance.

5) If you know a board member, do not make a point of it, yet do not hide it
Certainly you are not fooling him, and probably not the other members of the board. Do not try to take advantage of your acquaintanceship – it will probably do you little good.

6) Do not dominate the interview
Let the board do that. They will give you the clues – do not assume that you have to do all the talking. Realize that the board has a number of questions to ask you, and do not try to take up all the interview time by showing off your extensive knowledge of the answer to the first one.

7) Be attentive
You only have 20 minutes or so, and you should keep your attention at its sharpest throughout. When a member is addressing a problem or question to you, give him your undivided attention. Address your reply principally to him, but do not exclude the other board members.

8) Do not interrupt
A board member may be stating a problem for you to analyze. He will ask you a question when the time comes. Let him state the problem, and wait for the question.

9) Make sure you understand the question
Do not try to answer until you are sure what the question is. If it is not clear, restate it in your own words or ask the board member to clarify it for you. However, do not haggle about minor elements.

10) Reply promptly but not hastily
A common entry on oral board rating sheets is "candidate responded readily," or "candidate hesitated in replies." Respond as promptly and quickly as you can, but do not jump to a hasty, ill-considered answer.

11) Do not be peremptory in your answers
A brief answer is proper – but do not fire your answer back. That is a losing game from your point of view. The board member can probably ask questions much faster than you can answer them.

12) Do not try to create the answer you think the board member wants
He is interested in what kind of mind you have and how it works – not in playing games. Furthermore, he can usually spot this practice and will actually grade you down on it.

13) Do not switch sides in your reply merely to agree with a board member
Frequently, a member will take a contrary position merely to draw you out and to see if you are willing and able to defend your point of view. Do not start a debate, yet do not surrender a good position. If a position is worth taking, it is worth defending.

14) Do not be afraid to admit an error in judgment if you are shown to be wrong

The board knows that you are forced to reply without any opportunity for careful consideration. Your answer may be demonstrably wrong. If so, admit it and get on with the interview.

15) Do not dwell at length on your present job

The opening question may relate to your present assignment. Answer the question but do not go into an extended discussion. You are being examined for a *new* job, not your present one. As a matter of fact, try to phrase ALL your answers in terms of the job for which you are being examined.

Basis of Rating

Probably you will forget most of these "do's" and "don'ts" when you walk into the oral interview room. Even remembering them all will not ensure you a passing grade. Perhaps you did not have the qualifications in the first place. But remembering them will help you to put your best foot forward, without treading on the toes of the board members.

Rumor and popular opinion to the contrary notwithstanding, an oral board wants you to make the best appearance possible. They know you are under pressure – but they also want to see how you respond to it as a guide to what your reaction would be under the pressures of the job you seek. They will be influenced by the degree of poise you display, the personal traits you show and the manner in which you respond.

ABOUT THIS BOOK

This book contains tests divided into Examination Sections. Go through each test, answering every question in the margin. We have also attached a sample answer sheet at the back of the book that can be removed and used. At the end of each test look at the answer key and check your answers. On the ones you got wrong, look at the right answer choice and learn. Do not fill in the answers first. Do not memorize the questions and answers, but understand the answer and principles involved. On your test, the questions will likely be different from the samples. Questions are changed and new ones added. If you understand these past questions you should have success with any changes that arise. Tests may consist of several types of questions. We have additional books on each subject should more study be advisable or necessary for you. Finally, the more you study, the better prepared you will be. This book is intended to be the last thing you study before you walk into the examination room. Prior study of relevant texts is also recommended. NLC publishes some of these in our Fundamental Series. Knowledge and good sense are important factors in passing your exam. Good luck also helps. So now study this Passbook, absorb the material contained within and take that knowledge into the examination. Then do your best to pass that exam.

EXAMINATION SECTION

EXAMINATION SECTION
TEST 1

DIRECTIONS: Each question or incomplete statement is followed by several suggested answers or completions. Select the one that BEST answers the question or completes the statement. *PRINT THE LETTER OF THE CORRECT ANSWER IN THE SPACE AT THE RIGHT.*

1. After hooking down a train stop arm, a signal maintainer should FIRST notify the

    A. local tower
    B. train dispatcher
    C. Office of the Supervisor, Signals
    D. signal foreman

2. When a signal maintainer is opening an energized high voltage main, the electrical device to be opened FIRST is the

    A. fuse
    B. fused disconnect
    C. automatic transfer switch
    D. oil switch

3. When a signal maintainer is checking the fouling adjustment of a switch movement, the obstruction gage should be placed _____ inches from the tip of the point.

    A. 2   B. 4   C. 5   D. 6

4. Of the following, the item that is NOT part of the track circuit is the

    A. fusetron   B. track transformer
    C. resistor   D. home relay

5. A manipulation chart is used to determine the

    A. need to order signal equipment
    B. correct sequence of cars to be sent into the yard
    C. number of relays for a particular circuit
    D. correct combination of levers for a route

6. Of the following, the piece of signal equipment that is MOST likely to be under water if a section of track is flooded is the

    A. bootleg   B. track relay
    C. track repeater relay   D. track transformer

7. The tower horn signal that is used to notify the signal maintainer to contact the tower is

    A. short-short   B. short-long
    C. long-short   D. long-long

8. When the stop arm of an automatic train stop is in the clear position, it should be at LEAST _____ inch(es) below the top of the rail.

    A. 1/2   B. 1   C. 2 1/2   D. 3

9. Of the following, the BEST reason for using a single rail track circuit instead of a double rail track circuit is that the single rail track circuit

   A. can be used for a greater length of track
   B. is safer
   C. requires fewer insulated joints
   D. can be installed near contact rail

10. Of the following, the LOWEST acceptable value of insulation resistance for signal cable is _____ megohm(s).

   A. 1/2   B. 1   C. 2   D. 4

11. The EQUIVALENT resistance of two 10-ohm resistors connected in parallel is _____ ohms.

   A. 5   B. 10   C. 15   D. 20

12. A 5 to 1 step down voltage transformer has an input of 10 amperes at 100 volts. If losses are neglected, the MAXIMUM output of the transformer is _____ amperes at _____ volts.

   A. 50; 20   B. 10; 20   C. 2; 20   D. 2; 500

13. One ACCEPTABLE method of locking switch points, after the switch machine has been disconnected, is called

   A. tying   B. hooking   C. clamping   D. bracing

14. A megger is a testing device used to measure

   A. track current
   C. rail resistance
   B. track voltage
   D. insulation resistance

15. Normal inspection routines require that nickel-iron-alkaline batteries should be inspected for fluid level

   A. daily   B. weekly   C. bi-weekly   D. monthly

Questions 16-20.

DIRECTIONS: Questions 16 through 20 are based on the system of signal indication that is used on Division B (previously BMT and IND) and most of Division A (previously IRT).

16. A signal whose aspect is controlled only by the movement of a train is called a(n) _____ signal.

   A. home
   C. train order
   B. automatic
   D. marker

17. The signal aspect which requires a slow speed movement past the signal into the yard is

   A. red over red over yellow
   C. red over lunar white
   B. green over green over green
   D. yellow over yellow over yellow

18. A signal that gives ONLY a *stop and stay* indication is a(n) _____ signal.　　18.____

    A. automatic   B. home   C. marker   D. dwarf

19. A signal that displays either two horizontal red lights or two horizontal lunar white lights is called a _____ signal.　　19.____

    A. gap filler   B. marker
    C. train holding   D. train order

20. The signal aspect which means *proceed on main route and be prepared to stop at the next signal* is _____ over _____ .　　20.____

    A. yellow; green   B. yellow; yellow
    C. green; green   D. green; yellow

Questions 21-40.

DIRECTIONS: Questions 21 through 40 refer to the figure below, which shows standard one-block-overlap control lines for automatic block signals. Assume that the signal equipment is operating properly unless otherwise stated.

Questions 21 through 30 are for a territory where A.C. line controls are used.

21. A stick circuit is used to keep the _____ relay picked up.　　21.____

    A. distant   B. track repeater
    C. track   D. home

22. The energy supplied to the distant relay is　　22.____

    A. TB   B. LB   C. BX   D. BH

23. Signal 3 cannot display a green aspect when the　　23.____

    A. 3V train stop is clear
    B. 3HS relay is energized
    C. 3D relay is de-energized
    D. 2T relay is de-energized

24. Signal 2 always displays a red aspect when the _____ relay is de-energized.　　24.____

    A. 2HS   B. 3HS   C. 2D   D. 3D

25. Signal 4 displays a yellow aspect when it is receiving energy through a _____ contact of _____ relay.

    A. back; 4HS
    B. front; 4D
    C. front; 4T
    D. back; 4D

26. When a train is between signals 4 and 5, the signals that should be displaying a red aspect are _____ and _____ .

    A. 5; 6   B. 4;5   C. 3;4   D. 2;3

27. The retaining circuit for the 4V stop has a _____ contact of the _____ relay.

    A. front; 3D
    B. back; 3D
    C. front; 4T
    D. back; 4T

28. A contact in the control circuit of the 2HS relay is

    A. 1T   B. 3T   C. 1V   D. 2D

29. A contact in the control circuit of the 2D relay is

    A. 3HS   B. 2V   C. 2T   D. 2H

30. If the train stop 5V is in the tripping position due to a break in its control circuit, the number of signals that will display a red aspect is

    A. 0   B. 1   C. 2   D. 3

Questions 31 through 40 are for a territory where D.C. line controls are used.

31. The relay that is a repeater of the H relay and the clear position of the automatic stop is the _____ relay.

    A. DV   B. HS   C. D   D. HV

32. A contact in the control circuit of the 4H relay is

    A. 50V   B. 4HV   C. 5H   D. 5T

33. The energy for the control circuit of the 4H relay is

    A. TB   B. LB   C. VB   D. BH

34. A contact in the control circuit of the 2DV relay is

    A. 1HV   B. 3HV   C. 2H   D. 2T

35. If the 3HV relay is de-energized and the 3DV relay is energized, signal 3 _____ displays a _____ aspect.

    A. always; red
    B. sometimes; red
    C. always; yellow
    D. sometimes; yellow

36. If the 3HV relay and the 3DV relay are both energized, signal 3 _____ displays a _____ aspect.

    A. always; yellow
    B. always; green
    C. sometimes; yellow
    D. sometimes; green

37. The control circuit for the 2V all-electric stop includes a _____ contact of the _____ relay.

    A. front; 2H
    B. back; 2DV
    C. front; 2DV
    D. front; 2T

37._____

38. The energy for the control circuit of the 2DV relay consists of

    A. BX and LB
    B. VB and LB
    C. BX and VB
    D. LB and TB

38._____

39. A contact in the control circuit of the 2H relay is

    A. 2DV
    B. 2V
    C. 3HV
    D. 2D

39._____

40. As a result of an insulated joint breakdown at signal 5, the number of signals which would NOT display a green aspect is

    A. 2
    B. 3
    C. 4
    D. 5

40._____

KEY (CORRECT ANSWERS)

1. C	11. A	21. D	31. D
2. D	12. A	22. C	32. D
3. D	13. C	23. C	33. B
4. D	14. D	24. A	34. B
5. D	15. D	25. D	35. A
6. A	16. B	26. C	36. B
7. C	17. D	27. D	37. A
8. A	18. C	28. B	38. B
9. C	19. D	29. A	39. A
10. B	20. A	30. B	40. C

TEST 2

DIRECTIONS: Each question or incomplete statement is followed by several suggested answers or completions. Select the one that BEST answers the question or completes the statement. *PRINT THE LETTER OF THE CORRECT ANSWER IN THE SPACE AT THE RIGHT.*

1. A signal maintainer can be directed by his foreman to do all of the following EXCEPT   1.___

    A. break a seal on a relay
    B. operate an interlocking in an emergency
    C. invert a relay in order to close the contacts
    D. sectionalize a high voltage signal main

2. Assume that a number of conditions exist as the shift is changing.   2.___
   Of the following, a signal maintainer need NOT inform his relief that

    A. their telephone is out of order
    B. single track operation is in effect on part of their assigned area
    C. the track section is renewing rails on part of their assigned area
    D. the relief dispatcher is on duty

3. If a signal maintainer hooks down the automatic stop arm at an automatic signal display-   3.___
   ing a green aspect, the signal

    A. becomes dark immediately
    B. changes to red immediately
    C. changes to yellow
    D. remains green

4. When the specific gravity of the electrolyte in a battery has dropped to a certain value,   4.___
   the electrolyte must be replaced.
   This value of specific gravity at 60°F is

    A. 1.150   B. 1.160   C. 1.170   D. 1.180

5. Battery filler caps should be opened   5.___

    A. with a filler tool
    B. by hand
    C. with a special metal instrument
    D. with a wrench

6. On the latest signal installations, power for the signal system is USUALLY taken from the   6.___
   grounded neutral and phase wire #

    A. 1   B. 2   C. 3   D. 4

7. Traffic levers on interlocking machines should be painted   7.___

    A. white   B. red   C. black   D. blue

8. Spare levers on interlocking machines should be painted   8.___

    A. red   B. black   C. yellow   D. blue

9. Master levers on interlocking machines should be painted

    A. white   B. red   C. black   D. blue

10. The tower signal that is used to notify all the trains in an interlocking to come to an immediate stop is a horn blast sounding

    A. long-long   B. short-short
    C. short   D. long

11. Of the following, a condition that is LIKELY to cause a track relay to be sluggish when picking up is a

    A. broken stop arm
    B. wet roadbed
    C. sluggish home relay
    D. short in the wiring of the signal head

12. The connections between track relays and the running rails are USUALLY made of either No. 6 or No. _____ copper wire.

    A. 9 solid   B. 14 solid
    C. 9 stranded   D. 14 stranded

13. On a pushbutton type interlocking machine, a line of red lights indicates that a

    A. route has been set up
    B. switch is in transit
    C. signal is displaying a call-on aspect
    D. train is occupying the route

Questions 14-23.

DIRECTIONS: Questions 14 through 23 are to be answered on the basis of standard nomenclature and symbols.

14. The nomenclature for a reverse switch correspondence relay is

    A. RLP   B. RVP   C. RWC   D. RWZ

15. The ANS relay is used as a _____ relay.

    A. switch locking   B. route selection
    C. distant control   D. route agreement

16. The nomenclature for a relay used as a substitute for a lever in the reverse position is

    A. RWP   B. RWK   C. RLP   D. RFK

17. A call-on pushbutton stick relay is designated by the letters

    A. CO   B. CGDE   C. CC   D. COS

18. A time element relay is designated by the letter

    A. U   B. P   C. Q   D. C

19. The nomenclature for a 14-volt D.C. tower battery is 19.____

    A. TPOS   B. LB   C. TB   D. TT

20. The nomenclature for a contact rail indicating relay is 20.____

    A. CTP   B. Z   C. Y   D. CH

21. A signal cable is designated by the letter 21.____

    A. C   B. N   C. K   D. B

22. The switch emergency release relay is designated by the letters 22.____

    A. EM   B. ES   C. SS   D. SV

23. The letters ME are used to designate a(n) 23.____

    A. lever lock light   B. signal indicator light
    C. indication magnet   D. indication light

24. An emergency alarm location is indicated by a 24.____

    A. red light
    B. yellow and red striped sign
    C. red and white striped sign
    D. blue light

25. The device used to maintain tension in a cable messenger while the messenger is being repaired is called a 25.____

    A. come-along   B. mandrel
    C. rack   D. dynamometer

26. A 1500-ohm relay is to be operated at 12 volts D.C. from a 16.8-volt D.C. source. The CORRECT resistance to be placed in series with the relay should have a value of _____ ohms. 26.____

    A. 200   B. 300   C. 500   D. 600

27. To test for staggered rail polarity at an insulated joint, a low voltage test lamp should be placed across the joint. If there is staggered rail polarity, the lamp will 27.____

    A. flicker
    B. stay dark
    C. light and remain lit
    D. flash on and then go dark

28. When a signal maintainer connects a bank of lights to the contact rail, he should FIRST connect one lead to the _____ rail and then the other lead to the _____ rail. 28.____

    A. signal; contact   B. contact; signal
    C. negative; contact   D. contact; negative

29. According to standard flagging instructions, an ACCEPTABLE distance for the yellow lamps to be placed from the red lamp is _____ feet. 29.____

    A. 200   B. 400   C. 600   D. 800

30. According to standard flagging instructions, the LAST lamp to be removed from its fixed position on the trackway is the _____ lamp.

    A. yellow   B. white   C. red   D. green

31. If train speeds on a particular track are to be temporarily reduced to no more than ten miles per hour without the stationing of a flagman, the number of yellow lamps that should be placed on the track is

    A. 2   B. 3   C. 4   D. 5

32. MOST tracks relays in use are _____ position, _____ element, _____ relays.

    A. two; one; A.C.
    B. two; one; B.C.
    C. one; two; A.C.
    D. two; two; A.C.

33. The outboard bearing of a train stop SHOULD be lubricated with

    A. medium oil
    B. zero oil
    C. light grease
    D. graphol

34. The throw bar and locking bars of a switch machine SHOULD be lubricated with

    A. medium oil
    B. light grease
    C. zero oil
    D. graphol

35. Junction boxes are grounded to structural steel in order to

    A. prevent overloading
    B. protect against shock
    C. eliminate short-circuits
    D. complete the signal circuits

36. An interruption of two track sections may be caused by the

    A. A fuse having blown
    B. track feed fusetron having blown
    C. track relay having blown
    D. voltage on one of the track sections being too high

37. The leakage current in a track circuit affects the

    A. allowable wear of the running rails
    B. allowable length of the track circuit
    C. type of track transformer used
    D. type of track relay used

38. A typical signal head is equipped with _____ lamps.

    A. 3   B. 4   C. 6   D. 8

39. A fusetron is a combination of a fuse and a

    A. thermal cut-out
    B. relay
    C. switch
    D. resistor

40. On a pushbutton type interlocking machine, a line of white lights indicate that a
    A. signal is clear
    B. route has been set up
    C. switch is in transit
    D. train is occupying the route

KEY (CORRECT ANSWERS)

1. C	11. B	21. C	31. B
2. D	12. C	22. A	32. D
3. D	13. D	23. D	33. C
4. B	14. C	24. D	34. A
5. B	15. B	25. A	35. B
6. C	16. C	26. D	36. A
7. D	17. D	27. C	37. B
8. C	18. A	28. C	38. C
9. A	19. C	29. C	39. A
10. D	20. B	30. D	40. B

EXAMINATION SECTION
TEST 1

DIRECTIONS: Each question or incomplete statement is followed by several suggested answers or completions. Select the one that BEST answers the question or completes the statement. *PRINT THE LETTER OF THE CORRECT ANSWER IN THE SPACE AT THE RIGHT.*

1. Signal cable having an insulation resistance of less than 10 megohms should be remeggered approximately every 1.____

    A. month
    B. six months
    C. year
    D. two years

2. The train horn signal that is a warning to persons on or near the track is _____ sound(s). 2.____

    A. one long
    B. two short
    C. a succession of short
    D. two long

3. All of the following should be locked with a 1618 type lock EXCEPT doors of 3.____

    A. rooms that house air compressors
    B. rooms that house signal relays
    C. manholes that house signal power equipment
    D. rooms that house signal emergency material

4. An A.C. voltmeter should NOT be used to measure D.C. voltage because it will 4.____

    A. give an incorrect scale reading
    B. damage the circuit being tested
    C. get damaged
    D. alter the circuit being tested

5. On a GRS Model 5 switch mechanism, the main gear bearing should be lubricated with 5.____

    A. zero test oil
    B. graphol
    C. light grease
    D. heavy grease

6. On the WABCO Model A-10 switch mechanism, the main crank shaft, rollers, and bearings should be lubricated approximately every 6.____

    A. month
    B. six months
    C. year
    D. two years

7. On a lever-type interlocking machine, one of the items that is a BASIC part of the mechanical locking is the 7.____

    A. frog
    B. switch point
    C. relay
    D. dog

8. A manipulation chart is used to determine the 8.____

   A. correct combination of levers for a train move
   B. type of relays required for a particular circuit
   C. correct sequence of trains to be sent to the yard
   D. need to order signal parts

9. Signal heads are grounded to structural steel in order to 9.____

   A. protect personnel against electrical shock
   B. complete the signal circuit
   C. eliminate short-circuits
   D. prevent an improper signal aspect from being displayed

10. A sign with red and white stripes in the subway tunnel is a(n) _____ sign. 10.____

    A. stop
    B. no clearance
    C. employee loading platform
    D. exposed contact rail

11. When a signal maintainer is connecting a bank of lights to the contact rail, the proper practice for him to follow is to FIRST connect one of the leads to the _____ rail and then the other lead to the _____ rail. 11.____

    A. negative; contact   B. contact; negative
    C. signal; contact   D. contact; signal

12. A signal maintainer is requesting an ambulance for an injured person. Of the following, it is MOST important for him to give the 12.____

    A. location of the injured person
    B. cause of the accident
    C. name of the injured person
    D. name of the injured person's closest relative

13. Of the following, the lubricant that is NOT used on train stops is 13.____

    A. light grease   B. heavy grease
    C. zero test oil   D. light oil

14. The instrument that should be used to check the setting of time relays is a 14.____

    A. synchronous timer   B. reset timer
    C. gap timer   D. stroboscope

15. The device through which a track circuit wire is brought out from conduit for connection to the rail is called the 15.____

    A. junction box   B. bootleg
    C. splice   D. adapter

16. One reason for using matching transformers in signal track circuits is to   16._____

    A. eliminate the need for voltage taps on the track transformer
    B. prevent D.C. current from reaching the track transformer
    C. compensate for the voltage drop in the track circuit feeders
    D. prevent A.C. current from reaching the track relay

17. The number of marker conductors in a 7-conductor signal cable is   17._____

    A. 1   B. 2   C. 3   D. 4

18. According to the latest signal maintenance instructions, the stop arm head nearest to the   18._____
    running rail should be installed a certain horizontal distance from the gage side of this
    running rail.
    This distance is _____ inches.

    A. 4   B. 5   C. 6   D. 7

19. According to standard flagging instructions, the up and down movement of a yellow lamp   19._____
    is a signal to the motor-man to proceed at a

    A. minimum speed of 20 miles per hour
    B. maximum speed of 20 miles per hour
    C. normal speed expecting the next light to be green
    D. very slow speed and there is another flagman beyond

20. An automatic transfer switch will transfer the signal mains from normal to reserve power   20._____
    if the normal voltage dips below a critical voltage of _____ volts.

    A. 90   B. 100   C. 110   D. 120

KEY (CORRECT ANSWERS)

1.	C	11.	A
2.	C	12.	A
3.	C	13.	B
4.	A	14.	A
5.	C	15.	B
6.	A	16.	B
7.	D	17.	A
8.	A	18.	B
9.	A	19.	D
10.	B	20.	A

TEST 2

DIRECTIONS: Each question or incomplete statement is followed by several suggested answers or completions. Select the one that BEST answers the question or completes the statement. *PRINT THE LETTER OF THE CORRECT ANSWER IN THE SPACE AT THE RIGHT.*

1. The symbol for a track repeater relay is   1.____
   A. TP   B. T   C. TYP   D. TET

2. The symbol for a track transformer is   2.____
   A. TTBX   B. TBX   C. TT   D. T

3. The symbol for a signal indication light on an interlocking machine is   3.____
   A. ME   B. SV   C. HE   D. S

4. The symbol for 14 volt D.C. line battery is   4.____
   A. BX   B. TB   C. LS   D. LB

5. The symbol for a power off relay is   5.____
   A. PBS   B. PB   C. PO   D. PLX

6. The symbol for a normal switch repeater relay is   6.____
   A. NWC   B. NWK   C. NWP   D. NFK

7. The symbol for a train stop is   7.____
   A. V   B. TE   C. S   D. R

8. The symbol for an exit pushbutton stick repeater relay is   8.____
   A. PBS   B. X   C. XS   D. ES

9. The symbol for a time element relay is   9.____
   A. EM   B. TE   C. U   D. TM

10. The symbol for a reverse switch control relay is   10.____
    A. RWK   B. RWZ   C. RWR   D. RGP

11. According to standard flagging instructions, the FIRST lamp to be placed in its fixed position on the trackway is the _____ lamp.   11.____
    A. red   B. white   C. yellow   D. green

12. Which of the following statements regarding the tilting of a relay by a signal maintainer in order to facilitate the making of its contacts is true?   12.____
    It is

    A. allowed but the office of the supervisor, signals must be notified
    B. not allowed unless his foreman is present
    C. not allowed under any condition
    D. allowed but this action must be noted in the signal maintainer's log book

13. A fusetron is a combination of a fuse and a 13.____

   A. capacitor
   B. switch
   C. resistor
   D. thermal cut-out

14. Of the following, the MOST probable reason for two track relays dropping out when there is no train in the area is that the 14.____

   A. track transformer has shorted
   B. fusetron has blown
   C. A fuse has blown
   D. negative rail is broken

15. A signal maintainer is preparing to test a circuit with a multi-range ohmmeter. In order to prevent damage to the meter, he should check that the 15.____

   A. correct range is selected
   B. circuit is de-energized
   C. instrument is positioned face-up
   D. proper size resistor is placed in series with the ohmmeter

16. On lever-type interlocking machines, signal levers should be painted 16.____

   A. red   B. black   C. white   D. yellow

17. A voltmeter and an ammeter are being used to measure the power consumed by a certain resistor. The voltmeter reads 120 volts, and the ammeter reads 40 milliamperes. The power consumed is _____ watts. 17.____

   A. 0.192   B. 4.8   C. 560   D. 3000

18. The MAIN reason that signal rail joints are bonded is to 18.____

   A. reduce ballast resistance
   B. provide a high resistance path for the current going through the rail
   C. provide a low resistance path for the current going through the rail
   D. prevent steel dust from shorting the circuit

19. The equivalent resistance of a 6-ohm resistor and a 2-ohm resistor connected in parallel is _____ ohms. 19.____

   A. 1.5   B. 3   C. 8   D. 12

20. When the standard signal division test shunt is placed across the track rails at any point in a track circuit, the track relay should go to the full de-energized position. According to signal maintenance instructions, the resistance of this standard test shunt should be _____ ohms. 20.____

   A. 0.01   B. 0.03   C. 0.06   D. 0.10

KEY (CORRECT ANSWERS)

1. A
2. C
3. A
4. D
5. C

6. C
7. A
8. C
9. C
10. B

11. D
12. C
13. D
14. C
15. B

16. A
17. B
18. C
19. A
20. C

EXAMINATION SECTION
TEST 1

DIRECTIONS: Each question or incomplete statement is followed by several suggested answers or completions. Select the one that BEST answers the question or completes the statement. *PRINT THE LETTER OF THE CORRECT ANSWER IN THE SPACE AT THE RIGHT.*

Questions 1-20.

DIRECTIONS: Questions 1 through 20 refer to the figure below, which shows standard one-block overlap control lines for automatic block signals as used. Assume that the signal equipment is operating properly unless otherwise stated.

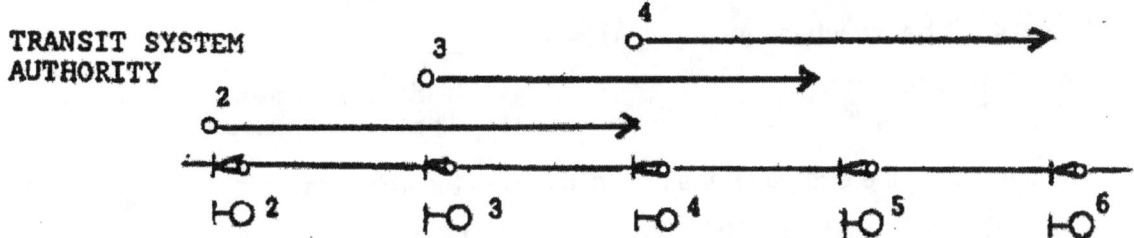

NOTE: Questions 1 through 10 are for a territory where A.C. line controls are used. Refer to the figure above when answering these questions.

1. When a train is between signals 5 and 6, the signals that should be displaying a red aspect are _____ and _____.

    A. 2; 3   B. 3; 4   C. 4; 5   D. 5; 6

    1.____

2. A contact in the control circuit of the 4D relay is

    A. 4V   B. 5V   C. 4T   D. 5T

    2.____

3. The stick circuit feature on the HS relay is necessary to

    A. hold the HS relay up
    B. maintain the proper voltage level
    C. insure that the HS relay will pick up promptly
    D. insure that there are no grounds causing a *false* pick up

    3.____

4. The control circuit for the HS relay includes a stop contact to check that the stop tripper arm is

    A. not broken
    B. clear for the next train
    C. in the tripping position after each train passes
    D. clear when the motorman keys-by a signal

    4.____

5. Energy for the retaining control of the automatic stop associated with signal 4 is taken through a _____ contact in the _____ relay.

    A. front; 4T   B. back; 4T
    C. back; 5HS   D. front; 4D

    5.____

17

6. Signal 4 will display a yellow aspect when it is receiving energy through the

   A. front contact of the 4D relay
   B. back contact of the 4D relay
   C. 4V stop contact
   D. front contact of the 4HS relay

7. Signal 4 will display a green aspect when it is receiving energy through the

   A. 4V stop contact
   B. front contact of the 4D relay
   C. back contact of the 4D relay
   D. front contact of the 4HS relay

8. Signal 4 will be red when the _____ relay is _____.

   A. 3HS; energized
   B. 3HS; de-energized
   C. 4HS; energized
   D. 4HS; de-energized

9. The symbol for the energy for the control circuit of the 4HS relay is

   A. TB
   B. BH
   C. LB
   D. BX

10. A contact in the control circuit of the 4D relay is

    A. 4HS
    B. 5HS
    C. 3T
    D. 3V

NOTE: Questions 11 through 20 are for a territory where D.C. line controls are used. Refer to the figure above when answering these questions.

11. The control circuit for the 4H relay includes a front contact of _____ relay.

    A. 3HV
    B. 3T
    C. 3DV
    D. 5T

12. A contact in the control circuit of the 4HV relay is

    A. 3DV
    B. 4DV
    C. 3H
    D. 4H

13. Signal 4 will display a green aspect when it is receiving energy through the

    A. front contact of the 4HV relay
    B. front contact of the 4DV relay
    C. front contact of the 4H relay
    D. 4V stop contact

14. A contact in the control circuit of the 4HV relay is

    A. 4V
    B. 5V
    C. 4T
    D. 5T

15. Signal 4 will display a red aspect when it is receiving energy through the _____ contact of the _____ relay.

    A. front; 4HV
    B. back; 4HV
    C. front; 4H
    D. back; 4H

16. When the DV relay drops out, the H relay remains picked up by a contact in the _____ relay.   16._____

    A. HV   B. H   C. DV   D. HS

17. The control circuit of the 4DV relay includes front and back contacts of the _____ relay.   17._____

    A. 3HV   B. 4HV   C. 4H   D. 3T

18. The control circuit for the DV relay is fed with _____ and _____ energy.   18._____

    A. LB; VB   B. BX; VB   C. BX; LB   D. BH; TB

19. The control circuit for the HV relay is fed with _____ energy.   19._____

    A. LB   B. VB   C. BX   D. TB

20. When the rear of a train is between signals 4 and 5, a signal that is displaying a yellow aspect is signal   20._____

    A. 1   B. 2   C. 3   D. 4

KEY (CORRECT ANSWERS)

1.	C	11.	D
2.	B	12.	D
3.	A	13.	B
4.	C	14.	A
5.	B	15.	B
6.	B	16.	B
7.	B	17.	B
8.	D	18.	A
9.	D	19.	B
10.	B	20.	B

TEST 2

DIRECTIONS: Each question or incomplete statement is followed by several suggested answers or completions. Select the one that BEST answers the question or completes the statement. *PRINT THE LETTER OF THE CORRECT ANSWER IN THE SPACE AT THE RIGHT.*

1. On lever-type interlocking machines, traffic levers should be painted 1.___
   A. white   B. red   C. blue   D. yellow

2. On lever-type interlocking machines, master levers should be painted 2.___
   A. red   B. white   C. yellow   D. green

3. On the GRS inductance type stop mechanism, the motor bearings should be lubricated with 3.___
   A. zero test oil
   B. dry graphite
   C. light grease
   D. heavy grease

4. If a signal maintainer has a telephone numbered B-3381 and he wishes to contact a person having a telephone numbered BI-229, he should 4.___
   A. dial 9, then dial BI-229 directly
   B. dial 1229 directly
   C. ask the operator to give him the desired number
   D. dial BI-229 directly

5. On the pushbutton type of control panel (NX and UR), when a switch is in transit, the area of the control panel showing the switches should flash 5.___
   A. white   B. red   C. green   D. yellow

6. On the pushbutton type control panel (NX and UR), a line of white lights means that a 6.___
   A. switch is in transit
   B. signal is displaying a call-on aspect
   C. route has been set up
   D. signal is set for fleeting

7. A signal that NEVER has an automatic stop is a(n) _____ signal. 7.___
   A. repeater
   B. home
   C. approach
   D. station time

8. The signal aspect which requires a slow train speed movement past the signal into the yard is _____ over _____ over _____. 8.___
   A. red; red; yellow
   B. yellow; yellow; red
   C. green; green; yellow
   D. yellow; yellow; yellow

9. The signal aspect which means *approach at the allowable speed and then proceed on the diverging route* is 9.___
   A. yellow over green with an illuminated S signal
   B. yellow over yellow over yellow
   C. red over red over yellow
   D. yellow over yellow with an illuminated S signal

10. A station time signal is used at certain locations to permit a train to

   A. leave a station even though the next signal aspect is red
   B. close in on a preceding train standing in a station
   C. leave a gap station even though it is ahead of schedule
   D. skip a station if it is traveling at a predetermined speed

11. A starting signal for a train at a terminal has three _____ lights.

   A. lunar white   B. green
   C. amber   D. blue

12. An indication of nickel-iron-alkaline batteries being overcharged is

   A. high terminal voltage
   B. warm cells
   C. the need to add water at less than 60-day intervals
   D. excessive gassing

13. The connections between track relays and the running rails are usually made of either No. 9 or No. _____ copper wire.

   A. 6 solid   B. 6 stranded
   C. 12 solid   D. 12 stranded

14. On the latest signal installations, power for the signal system is usually taken from the grounded neutral and the _____ phase wire.

   A. *A*   B. *B*   C. *C*   D. *D*

15. There are checking contacts in time relays to insure that these relays have

   A. finished the cycle of making their front and their back contacts
   B. returned to their full de-energized position after each operation
   C. made their front contacts
   D. accepted energy of the correct polarity

16. A signal maintainer is working in an area protected by caution lights, but he is not a member of the gang for whon the flagging protection was established.
   When a train approaches the signal maintainer, he should

   A. give a proceed signal to the motorman with a white lamp
   B. give a proceed signal to the motorman with a yellow lamp
   C. wave the train through by hand
   D. not give a proceed signal to the motorman

17. A signal maintainer discovers a condition requiring the immediate removal of third rail power.
   After he operates the emergency alarm box, he should NEXT notify

   A. the desk trainmaster
   B. his foreman
   C. the office of the supervisor, signals
   D. the fire department

18. All of the following are methods of securing the switch points after they have been disconnected from the switch machine EXCEPT

    A. blocking   B. tying   C. spiking   D. clamping

19. According to standard signal instructions, if a train stop arm is to be hooked down, the signal maintainer should notify the

    A. command center
    B. local tower
    C. train dispatcher
    D. office of the supervisor, signals

20. All of the following are found at emergency alarm locations EXCEPT a(n)

    A. emergency exit   B. blue light
    C. fire extinguisher   D. emergency telephone

KEY (CORRECT ANSWERS)

1.	C	11.	C
2.	B	12.	D
3.	A	13.	B
4.	D	14.	C
5.	B	15.	B
6.	C	16.	D
7.	A	17.	A
8.	D	18.	B
9.	D	19.	D
10.	B	20.	A

EXAMINATION SECTION
TEST 1

DIRECTIONS: Each question or incomplete statement is followed by several suggested answers or completions. Select the one that BEST answers the question or completes the statement. *PRINT THE LETTER OF THE CORRECT ANSWER IN THE SPACE AT THE RIGHT.*

Questions 1-8.

DIRECTIONS: Questions 1 through 8 refer to WX and UR interlocking typical circuits and relay sequences. Refer to the following sketch of the signals and switches when answering these questions.

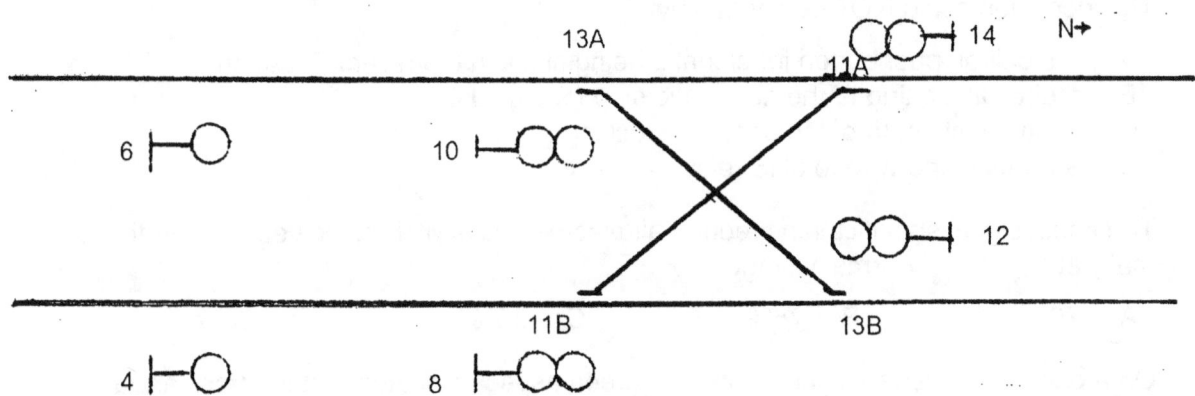

1. Number 10 entrance button is pushed. This picks up 10PBS relay. The NEXT relay that is picked up is

   A. 13ANN   B. 11ANN   C. 13RN   D. 11BNN

   1.____

2. After having pushed 10 entrance buttons, 12 exit button is pushed. 12XS relay is first picked up.
   The NEXT relay that is picked up is

   A. 11BNS   B. 13RS   C. 11ANS   D. 13RLP

   2.____

3. The number of sets of corresponding route selection relays that are picked up when making a move from signal 10 to signal 12 is

   A. 1   B. 2   C. 3   D. 4

   3.____

4. The number of sets of corresponding route selection relays that are picked up when making a move from signal 10 to signal 14 is

   A. 1   B. 2   C. 3   D. 4

   4.____

5. After having pushed 10 entrance and 12 exit button, the final line-up of picked up route selector relays will NOT include relay

   A. 13RS   B. 11ANS   C. 11BNS   D. 13ANN

   5.____

23

6. The 11NLP relay is picked up through the front contacts of 6.____

   A. 11ANN and 11ANS B. 11ANN and 13RS
   C. 13ANN and 11RS D. 11RS and 11RN

7. A relay contact that is NOT in the control circuit of 11NW2 relay is 7.____

   A. 11LS B. 11NWP C. 11RLP D. 11NWC

8. A relay contact in the white light circuit of 12K is 8.____

   A. 13RN B. 11BNN C. 11ANN D. 13ANN

9. When signal lever 6 of home signal 6 is reversed, home signal 6 continues to display red 9.____
   over red even though the track ahead is clear.
   This condition could NOT be caused by

   A. the call-on pushbutton for signal 6 being stuck in the reverse position
   B. faulty functioning of the automatic stop for signal 6
   C. faulty functioning of the approach locking circuit
   D. a break in the wire to 6HS relay

10. The latest signal specifications require all-electric D.C. switch machines to operate nor- 10.____
    mally at _____ of normal voltage.

    A. 70% B. 75% C. 80% D. 90%

11. On a one-block overlap signal system, a green aspect indicates that the track ahead is 11.____
    clear of trains for a MINIMUM of _____ block(s).

    A. 1 B. 2 C. 3 D. 4

12. Of the following four signal troubles reported about the same time, the one that is likely to 12.____
    cause the greatest delay to trains and should, therefore, be repaired. FIRST is a(n)

    A. automatic stop associated with the home signal controlling moves over a facing-point switch in regular use, which will not clear
    B. inoperative track circuit in automatic signal territory
    C. switch lever, controlling a trailing-point switch in regular use, jammed in the normal position
    D. home signal having a broken lens

13. Matching transformers are used in signal track circuits to 13.____

    A. compensate for the voltage drop in the track circuit fenders
    B. eliminate the need for voltage taps on the track transformer
    C. compensate for eddy current loss
    D. prevent D.C. propulsion current from reaching the track relay

14. One of the advantages of audio frequency track circuits is that they do NOT require 14.____

    A. insulated joints
    B. track relays
    C. rail connections
    D. as many personnel to operate the train

15. The number of marker conductors in a 7-conductor signal cable is   15.____
    A. 1   B. 2   C. 3   D. 7

16. The indication magnet *M* on the signal lever of the all-electric lever-type equipment has   16.____
    the same function as a certain relay on the NX and UR type equipment.
    This relay has the designation
        A. AS   B. ME   C. LS   D. R

17. A call-on signal is cancelled manually on an NX interlocking machine by _____ the   17.____
    _____ button.
    A. *pushing;* entrance   B. *pushing;* call-on
    C. *pulling;* entrance   D. *pulling;* call-on

Questions 18-23.

DIRECTIONS: Questions 18 through 23 refer to the all-electric lever-type interlocking machine.

18. Call-on pushbutton contacts are in the control circuit of the HS relay to   18.____
    A. prevent the HS relay from picking up as long as a call-on is displayed
    B. prevent a call-on signal from being displayed when the approach circuit is occupied
    C. prevent operation of the pushbutton from opening the HS control
    D. check that the pushbutton is not stuck in the reverse position

19. The switch detector circuit includes contacts from _____ relays.   19.____
    A. COS   B. route locking
    C. NWP   D. HS

20. The approach locking of an interlocking home signal does NOT include in its control circuit a   20.____
    A. front contact of an HS relay
    B. back contact of a COS relay
    C. back contact of a time element relay
    D. front contact of a track section in the approach to the signal

21. A tap is taken off the control circuit of the switch detector and cut-off relay for the _____   21.____
    light.
    A. ME   B. LE
    C. home signal   D. ZE

22. The HE light is tapped off the control circuit of the _____ relay.   22.____
    A. WR   B. DS   C. COS   D. HS

23. The controls for the HS relay are NOT selected through   23.____
    A. signal lever bands
    B. stop repeater relay contacts
    C. distant control relay contacts
    D. route locking relay contacts

Questions 24-28.

DIRECTIONS: The sketch below shows standard one-block-overlap control lines for automatic block signals as used. That is, each signal remains red while either of the two track circuits in advance is occupied, and each signal changes to green when the signal in advance becomes yellow.
Questions 24 through 28 are for territory where A.C. line controls or D.C. line controls are used. Refer to the sketch below when answering these questions.

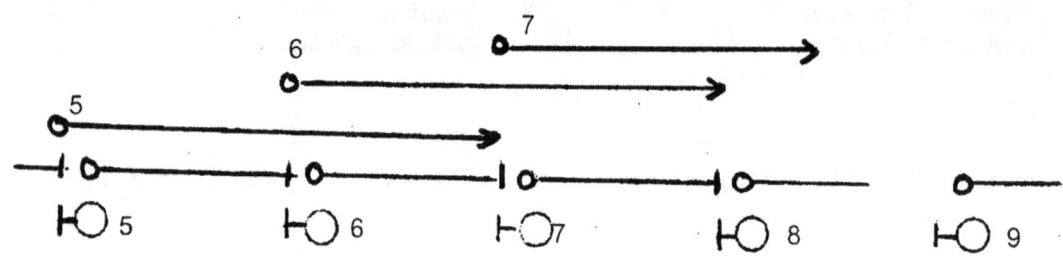

24. A contact in the control circuit for 50 relay has the nomenclature

   A. 5T   B. 6V   C. 5HV   D. 5V

25. In order to insure that the next signal is not red, the control circuit for 5DV relay receives energy through a front contact of _____ relay.

   A. 6HV   B. 6T   C. 5HV   D. 5T

26. The control circuit for 5HV relay includes a front contact of _____ relay.

   A. 6T   B. 5DV   C. 5H   D. 5T

27. The control circuit for 5H relay includes a _____ contact of _____ relay.

   A. back; 5DV
   B. back; 5HV
   C. front; 5HV
   D. front; 5DV

28. The control circuit for 5V all-electric stop in D.C. line control territory includes a _____ contact of _____ relay.

   A. back; 5HV
   B. front; 5T
   C. front; 5H
   D. front; 5HV

29. The part of a code control system that converts decimal data into binary data is the

   A. encoder
   B. decoder
   C. converter
   D. comparator

30. A voltmeter with a 100-microampere meter movement has a rating of

   A. 10,000 ohms/volt
   B. 1,000 ohms/volt
   C. 10,000 ohms.min.
   D. 1,000 ohms. max.

KEY (CORRECT ANSWERS)

1. B	11. C	21. B
2. A	12. C	22. D
3. C	13. D	23. C
4. B	14. A	24. B
5. D	15. A	25. A
6. A	16. A	26. C
7. D	17. C	27. D
8. B	18. D	28. C
9. C	19. B	29. A
10. C	20. A	30. A

TEST 2

DIRECTIONS: Each question or incomplete statement is followed by several suggested answers or completions. Select the one that BEST answers the question or completes the statement. *PRINT THE LETTER OF THE CORRECT ANSWER IN THE SPACE AT THE RIGHT.*

1. An A.C. voltmeter should NOT be used to measure D.C. because it will 1.____

   A. register zero
   B. get damaged
   C. pin below zero (read reverse)
   D. give an incorrect scale reading

2. Present day portable multimeters will OFTEN offer 2.____

   A. illuminated scales
   B. pushbutton scale changing
   C. built-in meter movement protection
   D. 50,000 ohms/volt

3. If an instrument has an accuracy of 3% full scale, the accuracy to which a quantity being measured can be read when the pointer is at 1/2 full-scale deflection is 3.____

   A. 3%   B. 1.5%   C. 6%   D. 9%

Questions 4-8.

DIRECTIONS: Questions 4 through 8 refer to proper flagging procedures for a signal maintenance gang working in an area protected by flagging.

4. When a flagman is setting up his position, the color of the first light he places on the track in its fixed position should be 4.____

   A. green   B. yellow   C. red   D. white

5. An ACCEPTABLE distance for the two yellow lamps to be displayed in approach to the flagman should be _____ feet. 5.____

   A. 75   B. 300   C. 600   D. 900

6. When flagging on a curve, an intermediate flagman should give a proceed signal to the motorman with a _____ lamp. 6.____

   A. white   B. green   C. yellow   D. blue

7. When it is necessary to reduce the speed of trains over a track adjacent to the track where a signal gang is working to not more than 10 miles per hour, without using a flagman, the MINIMUM number of yellow lights required is 7.____

   A. 1   B. 2   C. 3   D. 4

8. An ACCEPTABLE distance for the green lamp to be placed from the end of a work area is   8.____

   A. 400 feet
   B. as required by the office of the supervisor, signals
   C. at least the maximum length of a train permitted on the division
   D. dependent on the type of track in the area

9. If an expensive diamond ring is found on the tracks, it should be   9.____

   A. turned over to the transit police
   B. forwarded to the lost property office by a special messenger
   C. turned over to the transportation department
   D. turned over to the city police

10. The employee who carries a green lantern or baton and rides the head end of each train during single track operation over sections of track not signaled for two-directional operation is given the special name of   10.____

    A. flagman   B. handswitchman
    C. pilot   D. motorman instructor

11. When administering first aid to a signal maintainer suffering from shock as a result of falling off a ladder, it is MOST important to   11.____

    A. apply artificial respiration to the signal maintainer
    B. massage the signal maintainer in order to aid blood circulation
    C. prevent the signal maintainer from losing body heat
    D. notify the authority clinic

Questions 12-13.

DIRECTIONS: Questions 12 and 13 refer to the standard operating procedure for the derailment collision committee.

12. A department that is NOT represented in the derailment-collision field committee is the _____ department.   12.____

    A. maintenance of way
    B. power
    C. car maintenance
    D. rapid transit transportation

13. One purpose of the derailment-collision committee standard operating procedure is to   13.____

    A. start the trains moving as soon as possible
    B. reduce equipment destruction
    C. assist the desk trainmaster
    D. keep overtime to a minimum

14. According to standard signal instructions, signal cable is to be replaced when its insulation resistance is UNDER _____ megohm(s).   14.____

    A. 1   B. 5   C. 10   D. 20

15. The purpose for using unit code in the maintainer's weekly service report is to

    A. facilitate a *failsafe* system
    B. promote safety
    C. adapt the report for computer usage
    D. replace the equipment servicing record

16. The signal device master list has information necessary for filling out the maintainer's weekly service report. One piece of information NOT appearing on the master list is the

    A. device number
    B. job number
    C. section name
    D. supervisor's name

17. A signal maintainer has operated an emergency alarm box located at the end of a subway station.
    Power to the affected tracks should be restored ONLY upon orders from

    A. his foreman (signals)
    B. the office of the supervisor, signals
    C. the desk trainmaster
    D. the power department

18. A train horn signals sounds *long-short-long-short*.
    This means that the

    A. train crew needs assistance
    B. train needs a road car inspector
    C. train is making an irregular move
    D. signal maintainer should contact the tower

19. If a stop arm head does not meet certain specifications, it should be adjusted or replaced.
    The MINIMUM allowable horizontal distance from the side of stop arm head nearest the adjacent running rail to the gage of this running rail is

    A. 4 3/4"   B. 5"   C. 5 1/4"   D. 5 1/2"

20. An injury occurs to a signal maintainer that requires treatment by a physician.
    The accident need NOT be reported immediately by telephone to the

    A. transit authority clinic
    B. maintenance of way safety section
    C. maintenance of way control desk
    D. section supervisor's office

21. Of the following, the one that USUALLY requires a 1616-type lock is a

    A. yard bumper post signal
    B. door of a manhole that houses signal power equipment
    C. general railway signal switch machine cover
    D. signal case located within the confines of a properly locked signal enclosure

22. The index of the standard procedures manual is designed to locate subjects by _____ number.

    A. file   B. page   C. job   D. item

23. The MAXIMUM penalty that a signal maintainer can receive after a departmental hearing is

    A. loss of his job   B. 3 days' suspension
    C. 5 days' suspension   D. an official reprimand

24. When writing a report of an interruption to train service, an item that should NOT be listed as responsible for the delay is

    A. defective signal equipment
    B. lack of proper signal maintenance
    C. a defective fuse
    D. adverse weather conditions

25. Of the following statements, which one is NOT consistent with signal maintenance division policy?

    A. Reports must be submitted by signal maintainers on all interruptions to train service.
    B. It is necessary for the signal foreman to field investigate every delay to train service.
    C. A signal foreman's check on a maintainer's report of a train delay must be reported by telephone to the maintenance of way patrol office.
    D. A signal interruption report should include answers only to the questions of where, when, what, who, and why.

26. Signal cable having an insulation resistance of less than 10 megohms must be remeggered

    A. monthly   B. semi-annually
    C. annually   D. every two years

27. A signal maintainer takes a leave of absence because of a death in the family, but does not ask for advance approval. The signal foreman tells him after he returns to work that he should have asked in advance for the leave of absence.
The foreman's action was

    A. *bad;* according to the rules and regulations, a leave of absence under these circumstances doesn't require advance approval
    B. *good;* according to the rules and regulations, a leave of absence under these circumstances requires advance approval
    C. *bad;* this is a matter that should have been discussed with the union delegate
    D. *good;* the foreman discussed the situation with the signal maintainer but did not act harshly

28. After a signal maintainer has used up his sick leave, additional sick leave days are provided per sick leave year according to a schedule. The signal maintainer gets paid for these additional days at a percentage of his regular rate of pay.
This percentage is

    A. 60%   B. 70%   C. 80%   D. 90%

29. A signal maintainer is not satisfied with the results of a complaint he has presented to his foreman.
    He should write his appeal to the

    A. assistant supervisor (signals)
    B. supervisor (signals)
    C. superintendent (signals)
    D. impartial arbitrator

30. A signal foreman has received a complaint from a signal maintainer.
    He should communicate his decision to the signal maintainer within _____ after receiving the complaint.

    A. 24 hours   B. 48 hours   C. 1 week   D. 2 weeks

KEY (CORRECT ANSWERS)

1. D	11. C	21. B
2. C	12. B	22. A
3. C	13. B	23. B
4. A	14. A	24. D
5. C	15. C	25. B
6. C	16. D	26. C
7. C	17. C	27. A
8. C	18. A	28. A
9. B	19. A	29. C
10. C	20. A	30. B

TEST 3

DIRECTIONS: Each question or incomplete statement is followed by several suggested answers or completions. Select the one that BEST answers the question or completes the statement. *PRINT THE LETTER OF THE CORRECT ANSWER IN THE SPACE AT THE RIGHT.*

1. A signal maintainer reports to his foreman that a particular normal stop repeater relay picks up slowly although the voltage at the relay terminals is normal.
   The foreman should FIRST

   A. have this location checked for other defective relays
   B. check his records to see if this was reported previously
   C. order this relay to be replaced immediately
   D. go to the location and check it himself

   1._____

2. Standard signal section instructions specify that the setting of a time relay in the field must be checked with a(n)

   A. mechanical timer
   B. synchronous timer
   C. electronic timer
   D. stop watch

   2._____

3. If a test lamp lights when connected in parallel with a condenser across a suitable source of D.C., it is MOST probable that the condenser is

   A. of the rated capacity
   B. short-circuited
   C. fully discharged
   D. good

   3._____

4. The throw of a switch is always less than the throw of the switch machine to which it is connected.
   One LOGICAL reason for this is to permit

   A. the machine to gain momentum before moving the switch
   B. adjustment for the various sizes of switch
   C. adjustment for wear of the switch points
   D. the machine to be located at different distances from the rail

   4._____

5. The rating of two identical 20-ohm, 10-watt resistors connected in series is _____ ohms, _____ watts.

   A. 10; 10   B. 10; 20   C. 40; 10   D. 40; 20

   5._____

6. If there are two marker conductors in a multi-conductor signal cable, the total number of conductors in the cable is

   A. 5   B. 7   C. 19   D. 31

   6._____

7. If an induction-type time relay intended for use at 110-volts, 60-cycles is connected to a 55-volt, 25-cycle source, the relay will PROBABLY

   A. run slow
   B. run fast
   C. not even start
   D. operate the same as on 60 cycles

   7._____

8. The cross protection test on electropneumatic switch valves is made by

   A. interchanging the wires to the normal and reverse valves
   B. *punching* the three valves simultaneously
   C. operating the lock magnet with power off the valves
   D. shunting the KR or equivalent relay

9. It would be an indication of a careless signal maintainer if the foreman found

   A. insufficient oil in an automatic lubricator on the approach to a track curve
   B. a relay case in the subway without a padlock
   C. some lubricant had dripped to the roadway from an automatic stop outboard bearing
   D. the polar relay case at the end of an all electric unit-lever interlocking machine unlocked

10. The official instructions require that the MINIMUM time setting of mechanical time releases on signal levers must be _____ seconds.

    A. 15   B. 20   C. 25   D. 30

11. Your investigation of an accident would be MOST fruitful if you found the

    A. authority was not responsible
    B. signal section was not responsible
    C. exact cause of the accident
    D. responsibility could be pinned on a specific employee

12. A flashing white light in a switch segment on a route interlocking panel indicates that

    A. the switch has not responded to the route called for
    B. the switch has completed its motion
    C. a train is on the detector locking section
    D. there is an obstruction in the switch point

13. The standard shunt for testing track circuit sensitivity is five one-hundredths of an ohm. If only #12 A.W.G. wire (having a resistance of 1.6 ohms per 1,000 feet) were available, the proper length to use for the shunting sensitivity test would be

    A. 15' 6"   B. 23' 4"   C. 31' 3"   D. 50' 1 1/2"

14. Assume that a man was placed to flag trains while the men were working on the tracks. In accordance with the latest flagging instructions, the distance from the nearest point of work to the flagman must be AT LEAST _____ feet.

    A. 50   B. 75   C. 300   D. 500

15. A signal equipment failure which requires the use of the emergency release for the operation of a track switch through its controlling unit-lever is

    A. blown track fuse in the detector circuit
    B. jammed mechanical locking
    C. incomplete movement of the switch
    D. open indication circuit on an interlocked signal lever

16. One of the advantages claimed for audio frequency track circuits is that they do NOT require

    A. rail connections
    B. track relays
    C. insulated joints
    D. voltage adjustments

17. Assume that, as a consequence of a water main break, water floods to about an inch over the top of the ties in the subway.
    The MOST likely effect on the signal system will be that all

    A. submerged insulated joints must be replaced
    B. track fuses in the area must be replaced
    C. signals in the area will be red
    D. signals in the area will be dark

18. One feature of the signal system which CANNOT be classified as *failsafe* is that

    A. automatic stops go to the trip position when signal power goes off
    B. polarities of adjacent track circuits are staggered
    C. transformer-rectifier combinations are used to power D.C. line relays
    D. track relays are picked up when the tracks are clear of trains

19. A particular home signal in the subway controls moves over a trailing point switch. Assuming that the aspects of this signal are in accord with the latest practices, that it can display a call-on indication but does NOT have illuminated number plates, the TOTAL number of lamps in the signal is

    A. 10   B. 12   C. 14   D. 16

20. The MOST probable effect, on the signal system, of a broken negative return rail bond in an under-river tunnel will be that the track

    A. circuit involved will not operate reliably
    B. relay of the circuit involved will never pick up
    C. relay of the circuit involved will remain picked up when the rails are shunted
    D. circuit involved will have less D.C. in it

21. The leakage current of a track circuit can be correctly measured by connecting an ammeter across the _____-end fuse clips with _____ removed.

    A. feed; feed-end and relay-end fuses
    B. feed; only the feed-end fuse
    C. relay; relay-end and feed-end fuses
    D. relay; only the relay-end fuse

22. In automatic signal territory having one-block-overlap home controls, the number of signals that will change aspect when an insulated joint breaks down while no trains are in the area is

    A. 2   B. 3   C. 4   D. 5

23. A dog which is NOT found on either an all-electric or an electropneumatic unit-lever interlocking machine is a _____ dog.

    A. when   B. swing   C. locking   D. normal

24. If you suspect that a certain track resistor is too warm because it is partially short-circuited, a good way of checking your suspicions without interrupting the track circuit is by means of a properly connected

    A. A.C. ammeter   B. D.C. voltmeter
    C. wattmeter   D. ohmmeter

25. In making a report on the tripping of a train at a home signal indicating stop, the signal maintainer on the job would probably NOT be expected to report the

    A. name of the motorman
    B. condition of the signal equipment
    C. condition of the train wheels
    D. name of the towerman

26. A characteristic which is MOST desirable in a maintainer is

    A. a willingness to work overtime whenever asked
    B. the desire to keep aloof from other maintainers
    C. the ability to carry out assignments with a minimum of instruction
    D. insistence on doing an exactly specified amount of work each day

27. The restoring feature of a switch operating circuit functions to

    A. keep the switch point tight against the stock rail
    B. set up the circuit for the next move after each move is completed
    C. automatically restore the switch to its original position if there is an obstruction in the point
    D. restore the controlled switch to normal after the passage of each train

28. One indication of a possible broken negative rail on a two-track line in the subway would be

    A. unusually warm track resistors on a particular track circuit
    B. shunting of a track circuit on one track by trains on the other track
    C. failure of track relays on adjacent circuits to pick up
    D. tripping of a train due to an *unknown* cause

29. In addition to the usual clearance that must be provided on tangent track, a repeater signal in the subway MUST be so mounted so as to allow for

    A. wider column spacing   B. car center excess
    C. closer column spacing   D. car end excess

30. One purpose of the matching transformers used in modernized track circuits is to

    A. eliminate the need for voltage taps on the track transformer
    B. make the operation of longer track circuits feasible
    C. prevent D.C. propulsion current from reaching the track relay
    D. reduce the power required for track circuit operation

31. Allowing two seconds for the clearing of the automatic stop, and one-half second for relay operations, the time relay setting for a 540-foot track section where the allowable speed is 30 M.P.H. should be _____ sec.

    A. 9.8   B. 10.3   C. 12.8   D. 14.8

32. In some signal equipment cases, the relays are mounted on vibration pads, each pad consisting of two metal plates held apart by a number of compression springs.
    If a vane relay tilted and stuck due to corrosion failure of one or more of these compression springs after about 10 years of service, such relay failure should PROPERLY be charged to

    A. defective equipment
    B. improper maintenance
    C. excessive vibration
    D. high humidity

33. The nomenclature for two of the route selection relays used in route interlockings of the subway is

    A. NWP and RWP
    B. ARK and BRK
    C. NVP and RVP
    D. ANE and BNE

34. If a signal maintainer accidentally replaced a 25-watt, 64-volt signal lamp with a 25-watt, 120-volt lamp, the 120-volt lamp would

    A. light normally
    B. burn out
    C. burn brightly
    D. light dimly

35. After being tripped at a home signal, a train comes to a stop two-and-a-half car lengths past the signal.
    The number of times the stop arm will have been struck by trip arms on the train is

    A. 1   B. 2   C. 3   D. 4

36. The relay that is NOT likely to be needed at an S.T. signal location is a _____ relay.

    A. TP   B. HV   C. US   D. DV

37. If each strand of a signal wire has a diameter of 39 mils, the diameter of a wire made up of 7 such strands is NEAREST to _____ mils.

    A. 80   B. 115   C. 155   D. 270

38. Assume that you notice a light maintainer near your repair and renewal gang working on a live 600-volt circuit in a way that you believe is unsafe.
    It would be BEST for you to

    A. take no action because the man is not under your supervision
    B. take no action because you may be wrong in your belief
    C. ask the man if he is following standard lighting section procedure
    D. order the man to stop, and then tell him you are going to report him to his foreman

39. A maintainer learns that a certain interval is to be dropped.
    This means that

    A. the time interval between certain trains is to be reduced
    B. a certain train is to be taken out of service and no substitution made
    C. a certain train is to be reduced in length by a specified number of cars
    D. an additional train is to be placed in service in the interval between two regularly scheduled trains

40. A maintainer would properly consider it POOR supervisory practice for a foreman to consult with him on
    A. which of several repair jobs should be scheduled first
    B. how to cope with personal problems at home
    C. whether the neatness of his headquarters can be improved
    D. how to express a suggestion which the maintainer plans to submit formally

KEY (CORRECT ANSWERS)

1. C	11. C	21. A	31. A
2. B	12. A	22. C	32. B
3. D	13. C	23. D	33. D
4. A	14. B	24. D	34. D
5. D	15. A	25. C	35. C
6. C	16. C	26. C	36. A
7. A	17. C	27. A	37. B
8. B	18. C	28. A	38. C
9. B	19. B	29. D	39. B
10. B	20. A	30. C	40. A

EXAMINATION SECTION
TEST 1

DIRECTIONS: Each question or incomplete statement is followed by several suggested answers or completions. Select the one that BEST answers the question or completes the statement. *PRINT THE LETTER OF THE CORRECT ANSWER IN THE SPACE AT THE RIGHT.*

1. The emergency screw release on an interlocking machine is protected against unnecessary use by 1.____

    A. an alarm that cannot be silenced
    B. the control being in the trainmaster's office
    C. a lead seal
    D. a lock, with only the signal maintainer having a key

2. If the level of the electrolyte in several of the cells of an alkaline battery is found to be considerably below the level in the remaining cells, the maintainer should inspect these cells for 2.____

    A. bad connections   B. open terminals
    C. damaged plates   D. leaky containers

3. One advantage of the double rail track circuit as compared to the single rail track circuit is that the double rail track circuit 3.____

    A. operates at a much lower current drain
    B. needs fewer insulated joints
    C. can be used for greater lengths of track circuit
    D. requires less equipment

4. When connecting a track drill to operate from third rail power, the BEST practice is to connect to the 4.____

    A. third rail, then to the negative rail
    B. third rail and negative rail at the same time
    C. signal rail, then to the third rail
    D. negative rail, then to the third rail

5. In a written circuit, the symbol used to indicate a lever band made up from the reverse to the reverse indication position on a unit-lever interlocking machine is shown as 5.____

    A. (R)   B. (RD)   C. (RY)   D. (NR)

6. Safety considerations require that, when using the third rail jumper to supply power to a train, 6.____

    A. it should be handled by one man alone
    B. the third rail end should be connected first
    C. the shoe end should be connected first
    D. the motorman must keep power on until the shoe is on the third rail

39

7. The properly drawn symbol for a single crossover (on a track plan) is

A. B. C. D.

8. On the newest type pushbutton interlocking control panels, a yellow collar around a call-on button indicates that this signal is equipped with

   A. automatic route selection
   B. a stick feature
   C. a route request telephone
   D. a route annunciator

9. A signal maintainer need NOT inform his relief that

   A. single track operation is in effect
   B. the track section is renewing rails
   C. the relief signal foreman is on duty
   D. the telephone is out of order

10. Whenever it is necessary to sectionalize a high tension signal main, a signal maintainer must

    A. do exactly as instructed by supervision
    B. de-energize both feeders at the same time
    C. de-energize normal power before cutting-in reserve power
    D. first notify the trainmaster

11. With the track circuit unoccupied, the voltage at the relay end of the track circuit will be

    A. exactly half the feed-end voltage
    B. the same as the feed-end voltage
    C. 14 volts D.C.
    D. lower than the voltage at the track transformer

12. One term NOT used anywhere on the line to identify a D.C. power supply is

    A. VB   B. LB   C. TB   D. RX

13. Most signal heads are equipped with a means for determining the signal aspect from the rear of the signal.
    This device is called a

    A. back light   B. flag arm repeater
    C. distance repeater light   D. stop repeater light

14. If a test lamp lights when it is placed in series with a D.C. supply and a capacitor, the capacitor is PROBABLY

    A. shorted   B. fully charged
    C. open   D. fully discharged

15. According to official instructions, the outboard bearing of a train stop should be lubricated with

    A. light grease as required
    B. light grease monthly
    C. zero oil monthly
    D. zero oil as required

16. Standard signal instructions require that Nickel - Iron- Alkaline batteries have a voltage across each individual cell's terminals of _____ volts.

    A. 1.22   B. 1.44   C. 1.66   D. 1.88

17. When a lever in a unit-lever interlocking machine is moved to reverse a switch, the actual locking of conflicting levers takes place while the lever is being moved from

    A. normal to normal indication
    B. normal indication to center
    C. center to reverse indication
    D. reverse indication to full reverse

18. On unit-lever interlocking machines, signal maintainers are usually NOT permitted to disconnect the mechanical locking from a switch lever because

    A. this will prevent other levers from operating
    B. part of the safety features of the interlocking will be defeated
    C. this will damage the lever guide
    D. this cannot be done easily by one man alone

19. A 1000 ohm relay is to be operated at 12 volts D.C. from a 16.8 volt D.C. supply. The correct size resistor to be placed in series with the relay is _____ ohms.

    A. 300   B. 350   C. 400   D. 480

20. The symbol HY stands for home

    A. slotting   B. signal   C. yard   D. caution

21. Signal maintainers are always cautioned to check on the location of trains before adjusting or servicing any signal equipment primarily to prevent

    A. damage to signal equipment
    B. tripping of a train
    C. electrical shock
    D. wrong routing of a train

22. One fail-safe feature incorporated in track circuit design is

    A. staggered insulated joint polarity
    B. high current bootleg connections
    C. multi-contact relays
    D. high resistance shunting

23. If a switch machine must be disconnected from the switch points, the FIRST person to be informed is the

    A. towerman
    B. trainmaster
    C. dispatcher
    D. supervisor, signals

24. The distance from the gauge of rail to the center-line of a stop arm is

    A. 6 1/4"   B. 7 1/4"   C. 8 1/4"   D. 9 1/4"

25. The device through which a track circuit wire is brought out from conduit or trunking for connection to the rail is called the

    A. S connector
    B. signal rail bond
    C. shunt rail adapter
    D. bootleg

26. The whistle signal for a signal maintainer is

    A. long-short
    B. long-long
    C. short-short
    D. short-long

27. In the clear position, the stop arm should be AT LEAST _____ inch(es) _____ ball of rail.

    A. 2 1/2; above
    B. 1/2; above
    C. 2 1/2; below
    D. 1/2; below

Questions 28-40.

DIRECTIONS: Questions 28 through 40, inclusive, are based on the sketches below showing a series of automatic signals along an express track in the subway, and the control circuits for signal 26. All signals have standard one-block-overlap home controls, and there are no time controls or overlapped distant controls; that is, each signal remains red while either of the two track circuits in advance is occupied, and each signal changes to green when the signal in advance becomes yellow. The arrangement of equipment in the signal cases at each signal location is standard.

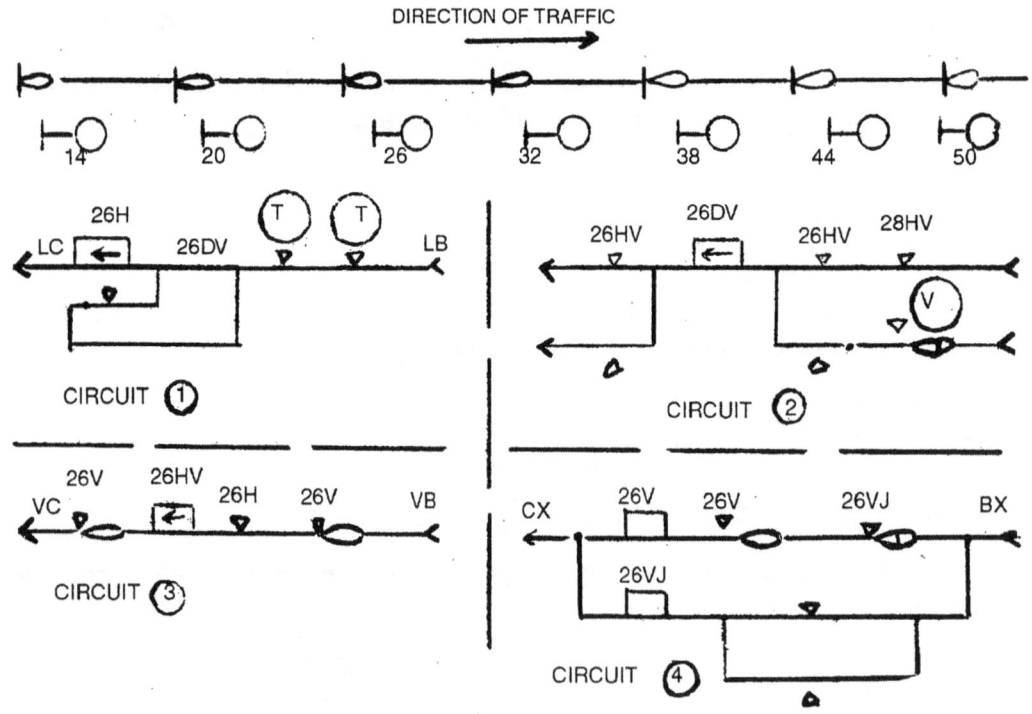

28. Assume that the track is unoccupied and that there is an open wire in the home control of signal #32.
   This open circuit is indicated by the fact that

   A. only signal #32 is red
   B. both signals #26 and #32 are red
   C. both signals #32 and #38 are red
   D. signal #32 is yellow and signal #26 is red

29. Assume that the track is unoccupied, but due to a break in the operating circuit the automatic stop arm at signal #38 remains in the trip position.
   This trouble is indicated by the fact that signal(s)

   A. #26, #32, and #38 will be red and signal #20 will be yellow
   B. #38 will be yellow and signal #32 will be red
   C. #38 will be red and signal #32 will be yellow
   D. #32 and #38 will be red and signal #26 will be yellow

30. If the distant relay for signal #26 is stuck in its de-energized position, the result will be that signal #26 will _____ display _____.

   A. *never*; green   B. *always*; yellow
   C. *always*; green   D. *never*; yellow

31. For circuit ①, the two track relays that would be used are _____ T and _____ T.

   A. 14; 20   B. 20; 26   C. 26; 32   D. 32; 38

32. Circuit ① shows the _____ control.

   A. distant   B. home signal
   C. home signal clear stop   D. electric stop

33. For circuit ②, the nomenclature that is omitted from one of the devices is _____ V.

   A. 20   B. 26   C. 32   D. 38

34. The proper nomenclature for the energy supply in circuit ② is

   A. LB & VB   B. LB & BX   C. BX & BH   D. BH & VD

35. The voltage level of LB is _____ volts.

   A. 8   B. 14   C. 24   D. 55

36. In circuit ④, a contact in the retaining circuit is the _____ contact.

   A. track relay   B. distant relay
   C. lock relay   D. stop

37. Circuit ③ shows the _____ control.

   A. distant   B. home signal
   C. home signal clear stop   D. electric stop

38. Assume that at a time when signal #44 is green, a train has stopped with its front end between signals #38 and #44 and its rear end between signals #26 and #32.
Under these conditions, the number of automatic stops for which the retaining circuits are completed is

   A. 1   B. 2   C. 3   D. 4

39. Under the conditions of Question No. 38, the number of signals displaying *red* is

   A. 1   B. 2   C. 3   D. 4

40. Assume that signals #14, #20, and #26 are green; signal #32 is yellow; and signals #38, #44, and #50 are red. This condition would be brought about by a train on the track with its rear end

   A. past signal #50
   B. between signals #44 and 50
   C. between signals #38 and 44
   D. between signals #32 and 38

KEY (CORRECT ANSWERS)

1. C	11. D	21. B	31. C
2. D	12. D	22. A	32. B
3. C	13. A	23. D	33. B
4. D	14. A	24. B	34. A
5. B	15. B	25. D	35. B
6. C	16. B	26. A	36. A
7. B	17. A	27. D	37. C
8. C	18. B	28. A	38. C
9. C	19. C	29. C	39. D
10. A	20. A	30. A	40. B

TEST 2

DIRECTIONS: Each question or incomplete statement is followed by several suggested answers or completions. Select the one that BEST answers the question or completes the statement. *PRINT THE LETTER OF THE CORRECT ANSWER IN THE SPACE AT THE RIGHT.*

1. The MAIN reason that signal rails are bonded between insulated joints is to 1.____

   A. provide a high resistance path
   B. provide a low resistance path
   C. reduce ballast resistance
   D. replace impedance bonds

2. The piece of signal equipment MOST likely to be under water if a broken water main floods the subway is the 2.____

   A. track transformer
   B. track relay
   C. switch circuit controller
   D. track repeater relay

3. One color of light NOT used to convey information at the latest type of pushbutton interlocking control panel is 3.____

   A. red   B. blue   C. green   D. white

4. The standard nomenclature for the normal switch correspondence relay is 4.____

   A. NWR   B. NWZ   C. NWP   D. NWC

5. An automatic transfer switch will transfer the signal mains from normal to reserve power if the normal voltage dips below a critical voltage of _____ volts. 5.____

   A. 70   B. 90   C. 110   D. 120

6. The MOST important reason for blocking out dust and moisture from subway signal cases is to prevent 6.____

   A. unsanitary working conditions
   B. corrosion of contacts and wires
   C. decay of prints
   D. unnecessary painting

7. S.T. signals are generally used when it is desired to 7.____

   A. limit speed of trains on a long downgrade
   B. limit speed of trains through an interlocking
   C. allow trains to *close-in* in approach to an occupied station
   D. reduce speed of trains on curves

8. The proper lantern signal to give a motorman to proceed past an out-of-service automatic signal in the subway is waving a 8.____

   A. green lantern across the track
   B. white lantern across the track

45

C. red lantern up and down
D. white lantern up and down

9. A signal maintainer would use a megger to test

    A. track current
    B. ballast resistance
    C. insulation resistance
    D. track voltage

10. A manipulation chart is used to determine the

    A. proper operating procedure for car equipment
    B. correct combination of levers for a route
    C. correct sequence of cars to be sent into the yard
    D. schedule of intervals at a gap point

11. When only one train at a time is permitted into a specific track area, this type of operation is called

    A. skip-stop
    B. diverging routing
    C. absolute block
    D. flexible interval

12. On level tangent track, two yellow lanterns are placed 800 feet from a flagman guarding a work gang. According to standard flagging instructions, if there are no unusual conditions such as a station in between,

    A. the lanterns are too far away from the flagman
    B. the lanterns are properly placed
    C. only one yellow lantern is required
    D. the lanterns are too close to the flagman

13. Standard flagging instructions require that the minimum distance a flagman is to place his portable trip and red lamp from the work area is

    A. 50 feet
    B. 75 feet
    C. two car lengths
    D. one-half car length

14. The reverse position of a switch lever on an electro-pneumatic conventional interlocking machine is

    A. pulled all the way out
    B. pushed all the way in
    C. pointing to the left
    D. pointing to the right

15. The normal position of a switch lever on an all-electric conventional interlocking machine is

    A. pulled all the way out
    B. pushed all the way in
    C. pointing to the left
    D. pointing to the right

16. Safety considerations prohibit the use of carbon tetra-chloride fire extinguishers on fires in the subway MAINLY because of the

    A. difficulty in refilling the extinguisher
    B. danger of damage to equipment
    C. noxious fumes given off
    D. shock hazard involved

17. One term that can properly be applied to the mechanical locking of a unit lever interlocking machine is

    A. frog B. apron C. bootleg D. dog

18. If it is desired to stop all trains within the interlocking limits, the towerman should sound, on the tower horn, _____ blast(s).

    A. two long
    B. a rapid succession of short
    C. one short
    D. one long

19. Wire tags do NOT show the wire

    A. size
    B. location
    C. destination
    D. designation

20. The symbol for a front contact of a normally de-energized relay would be shown on written circuits as

    A. B. C. D.

21. The instrument that should be used to check the setting of time relays is a _____ timer.

    A. synchronous
    B. reset
    C. solenoid
    D. gap

22. One condition NOT likely to cause a track relay to be sluggish in picking up is a

    A. faulty insulated joint
    B. broken stop arm
    C. low feed and voltage
    D. wet roadbed

23. One dangerous condition that can arise in a 4-track subway area with single rail track circuits is that

    A. removal of a negative rail may not cause any track relay to drop
    B. breakdown of two consecutive insulated joints will prevent proper shunting of track circuits
    C. bonding of rails will cause excessive propulsion current to flow in the signal rail
    D. stray currents from one track can affect an adjacent track

24. According to standard instructions, the shunting sensitivity of track circuits should be checked

    A. annually
    B. semi-annually
    C. quarterly
    D. monthly

25. The most important reason for NOT connecting a bank of lamps to the signal rail is

    A. shock hazard
    B. insulated joint breakdown
    C. excessive current drain
    D. lamps would glow dimly

26. A signal maintainer, when checking the fouling adjustment of a switch movement, should place the obstruction gage

A. opposite the basket rod
B. 6 inches from the tip of the point
C. at tip of the point
D. 3 1/2 inches from the tip of the point

27. According to the rules, a signal maintainer may operate an interlocking plant in an emergency provided that he   27._____

    A. has been qualified by the towerman
    B. has worked the interlocking regularly
    C. is ordered to do so by the dispatcher
    D. receives permission from signal supervision

Questions 28-33.

DIRECTIONS: Questions 28 through 33, inclusive, are based on the sketches below. The right-hand sketch shows the nomenclature on the wires of a cable entering a signal case, and the left-hand sketch shows the end view of the cable in the case as it would be before connecting up. Refer to these sketches in answering these questions. Use the letters B, F, C, etc. shown in the left-hand sketch when identifying conductors in that sketch.

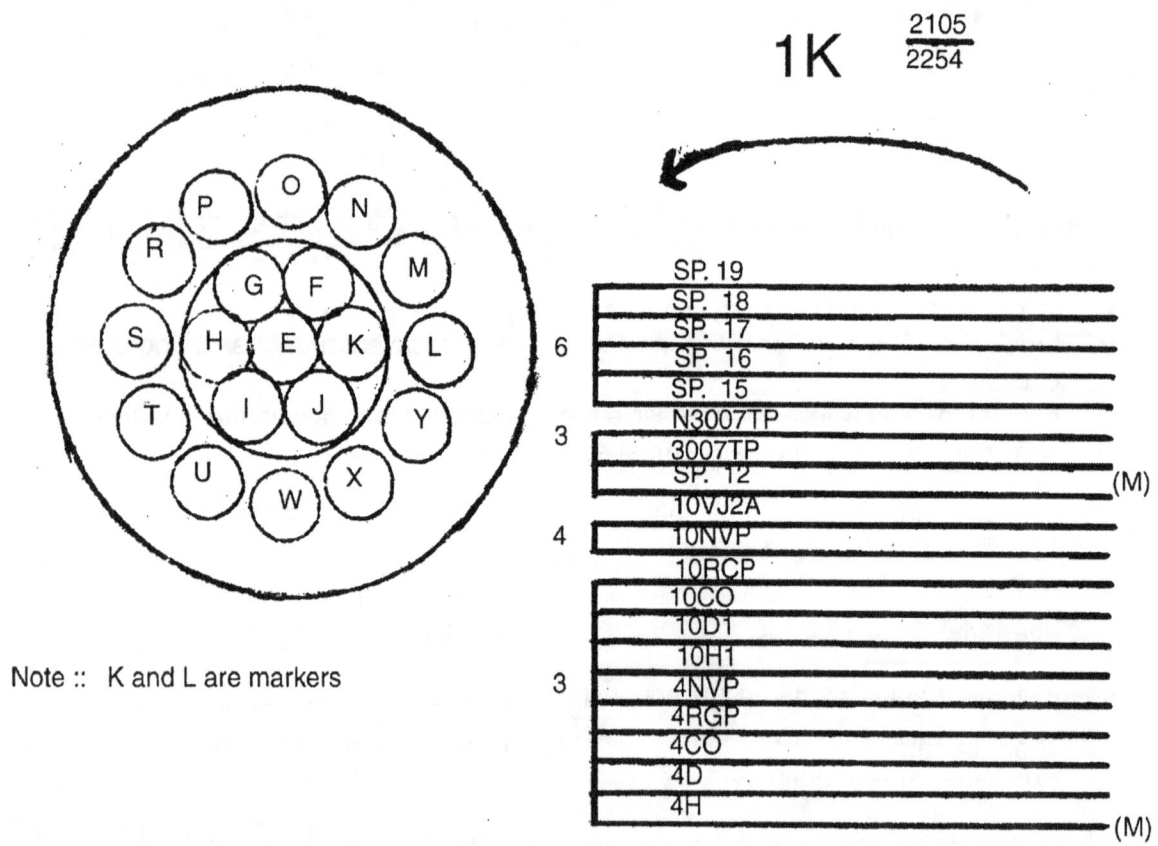

Note :: K and L are markers

28. The number of spare conductors that go to terminal board #3 from cable 1K is   28._____

    A. 1   B. 2   C. 3   D. 5

29. The nomenclature of wire E in the left-hand sketch is   29.____

   A. 4H   B. SP.19   C. 3007TP   D. 10NVP

30. It is clear from the nomenclature that signal 4 is a _____ signal.   30.____

   A. rear-home   B. train order
   C. home   D. marker

31. The nomenclature of wire Y in the left-hand sketch is   31.____

   A. 4H   B. 3007TP   C. N3007TP   D. SP.12

32. The conductors in cable 1K are counted _____ starting at the _____.   32.____

   A. *clockwise;* center conductor
   B. *clockwise;* markers
   C. *counterclockwise;* center conductor
   D. *counterclockwise;* outer marker

33. One of the marker wires in cable 1K has the nomenclature   33.____

   A. 3007TP   B. SP.19   C. 4D   D. SP.12

34. A maintainer, in routine checking of a particular signal junction box, finds that, according   34.____
    to the tags, several of the wires are on different terminals from those indicated on the
    blueprint.
    He should

   A. mark the blueprint to agree with what he found
   B. make no changes but notify the signal office promptly
   C. rearrange the wires to agree with the blueprints
   D. test out each circuit and make the necessary changes

35. The amount of leakage current in a track circuit depends LEAST on the   35.____

   A. extent of wear of the running rails
   B. length of the track circuit
   C. type of track construction
   D. condition of the ballast

36. If a signal maintainer hooks down the automatic stop arm at a green automatic signal,   36.____
    the signal will

   A. become dark
   B. change to yellow
   C. change to red
   D. continue to display green

37. In accordance with standards, the properly drawn symbol for a normally open contact of   37.____
    a pushbutton is

38. Where traffic may be in either direction, the master lever of a unit-lever interlocking machine is painted

    A. blue   B. black   C. red   D. white

39. The standard nomenclature for the reverse switch repeater relay is

    A. RWR   B. RWZ   C. RWP   D. RWC

40. G.T. signals are GENERALLY used when it is desired to

    A. limit speed of trains on a long downgrade
    B. allow trains to *close-in* in approach to an occupied station
    C. limit speed of trains through an interlocking
    D. reduce speed of trains on upgrade

KEY (CORRECT ANSWERS)

1. B	11. C	21. A	31. D
2. C	12. A	22. B	32. D
3. B	13. B	23. A	33. A
4. D	14. C	24. D	34. B
5. B	15. B	25. A	35. A
6. B	16. C	26. B	36. D
7. C	17. D	27. D	37. C
8. D	18. D	28. A	38. D
9. C	19. A	29. B	39. C
10. B	20. B	30. C	40. A

TEST 3

DIRECTIONS: Each question or incomplete statement is followed by several suggested answers or completions. Select the one that BEST answers the question or completes the statement. *PRINT THE LETTER OF THE CORRECT ANSWER IN THE SPACE AT THE RIGHT.*

1. The MOST important reason for blocking out dust and moisture from subway signal cases is to prevent

    A. corrosion of contacts and wires
    B. decay of prints
    C. unnecessary painting
    D. unsanitary working conditions

2. The equivalent resistance of two 6-ohm track resistors connected in parallel is _____ ohms.

    A. 12   B. 6   C. 3   D. 1.5

3. The piece of signal equipment MOST likely to be under water if a broken water main floods the subway is the

    A. track relay
    B. track transformer
    C. track repeater relay
    D. switch circuit controller

4. The device through which a track circuit wire is brought out from conduit for connection to the rail is called the

    A. signal rail bond   B. shunt rail adapter
    C. S connector   D. bootleg

5. One fail-safe feature incorporated in track circuit design is

    A. high current bootleg connections
    B. staggered insulated joint polarity
    C. high resistance shunting
    D. multi-contact relays

6. In the clear position, the stop arm should be AT LEAST _____(es) _____ top of rail.

    A. 1/2; above   B. 1/2; below   C. 2 1/2; above   D. 2 1/2; below

7. The whistle or horn signal for a signal maintainer is

    A. short-long   B. long-short
    C. long-long   D. short-short

8. The MAIN reason that signal rails are bonded at rail joints is to

    A. provide a low resistance path
    B. provide a high resistance path
    C. reduce ballast resistance
    D. replace impedance bonds

9. A manipulation chart is used to determine the   9._____
    A. proper operating procedure for car equipment
    B. correct sequence of cars to be sent into the yard
    C. correct combination of levers for a route
    D. schedule of intervals at a gap point

10. On unit-lever interlocking machines, signal maintainers are usually NOT permitted to dis-   10._____
    connect the mechanical locking from a switch lever because
    A. this cannot be done easily by one man alone
    B. this will prevent other levers from operating
    C. this will damage the lever guide
    D. part of the safety features of the interlocking will be defeated

11. According to the rules, a signal maintainer may operate an interlocking plant in an emer-   11._____
    gency provided that he
    A. is ordered to do so by the dispatcher
    B. receives permission from the office of the supervisor of signals
    C. has worked the interlocking regularly
    D. has been qualified by the towerman

12. One dangerous condition that can arise in a 4-track subway area with single rail track cir-   12._____
    cuits is that
    A. bonding of rails will cause excessive propulsion current to flow in the signal rail
    B. removal of a negative rail may not cause any track relay to drop
    C. breakdown of two consecutive insulated joints will prevent proper shunting of track circuits
    D. the signal will always stay green if the stop arm is hooked down

13. The instrument that should be used to check the setting of time relays is a _____ timer.   13._____
    A. reset   B. synchronous
    C. gap   D. solenoid

14. According to standard instructions, the shunting sensitivity of track circuits should be   14._____
    checked
    A. semi-annually   B. quarterly
    C. monthly   D. annually

15. A signal maintainer, when checking the fouling adjustment of a switch movement, should   15._____
    place the obstruction gage
    A. 6 inches from the tip of the point
    B. at the tip of the point
    C. 3 1/2 inches from the tip of the point
    D. opposite the basket rod

16. Signal maintainers are always cautioned to check on the location of trains before adjust-   16._____
    ing or servicing any signal equipment PRIMARILY to prevent
    A. electrical shock
    B. wrong routing of a train

    C. damage to signal equipment
    D. tripping of a train

17. If a signal maintainer hooks down the automatic stop arm at a green automatic signal, the signal will   17.____

    A. change to yellow
    B. continue to display green
    C. become dark
    D. change to red

18. According to official instructions, the outboard bearing of a train stop should be lubricated with   18.____

    A. zero oil as required   B. light grease as required
    C. light grease monthly   D. zero oil monthly

19. Most signal heads are equipped with a means for determining the signal aspect from the rear of the signal.   19.____
This device is called a

    A. distance repeater light   B. stop repeater light
    C. flag arm repeater   D. back light

20. With the track circuit unoccupied, the voltage at the relay end of the track circuit will be   20.____

    A. higher at the relay terminals than at the rails
    B. exactly half the feed-end voltage
    C. lower than the voltage at the track transformer
    D. the same as the feed-end voltage

21. If a test lamp lights when it is placed in series with a D.C. supply and a capacitor, the capacitor is PROBABLY   21.____

    A. open   B. fully discharged
    C. shorted   D. fully charged

22. The amount of leakage current in a track circuit depends LEAST on the   22.____

    A. type of track construction
    B. extent of wear of the running rails
    C. condition of the ballast
    D. length of the track circuit

23. One condition NOT likely to cause a track relay to be sluggish in picking up is a   23.____

    A. faulty insulated joint   B. broken stop arm
    C. low feed-end voltage   D. wet roadbed

24. G.T. signals are GENERALLY used when it is desired to   24.____

    A. limit speed of trains through an interlocking
    B. limit speed of trains on a long downgrade
    C. reduce speed of trains on upgrade
    D. allow trains to *close-in* in approach to an occupied station

Questions 25-29.

DIRECTIONS: Questions 25 through 29 are based on the system of signal indications referred to in the paragraph below. Refer to this paragraph when answering these questions.

The entire transit system, except for a few instances, utilizes a system of interlocking signal indications that requires a train to come to a full stop before passing a home signal having a red aspect.

25. The signal aspect which means proceed with caution on diverging route prepare to stop at next signal is

   A. green over green
   B. yellow over green
   C. yellow over yellow
   D. green over yellow

26. The signal aspect which means proceed with caution on main route prepare to stop at next signal is

   A. green over yellow
   B. yellow over green
   C. yellow over yellow
   D. green over green

27. The signal aspect for a call-on is

   A. red over red over yellow
   B. yellow over yellow over yellow
   C. red over red over green
   D. yellow over yellow over green

28. The signal aspect which means proceed on diverging route is

   A. green over yellow
   B. yellow over yellow
   C. yellow over green
   D. green over green

29. The signal aspect which means proceed on main route is

   A. green over yellow
   B. yellow over yellow
   C. yellow over green
   D. green over green

30. One inspection item NOT made monthly on an alkaline storage battery is

   A. cell voltage of at least six cells
   B. specific gravity of electrolyte
   C. condition of terminals and terminal nuts
   D. condition of filler valve body

Questions 31-40.

DIRECTIONS: Questions 31 through 40 are based on generally accepted transit system nomenclature.

31. The nomenclature for the normal switch correspondence relay is

   A. NWR   B. NWC   C. NWP   D. NWZ

32. The nomenclature HY stands for home

    A. caution relay
    B. relay (slotting)
    C. signal relay
    D. yard relay

33. The letters used as a prefix for positive A.C. energy are

    A. BX
    B. BH
    C. LB
    D. VB

34. The nomenclature for the distant control relay is

    A. DV
    B. H
    C. HS
    D. COS

35. The nomenclature for the 14 volt D.C. line battery is

    A. LS
    B. L
    C. LE
    D. LB

36. The nomenclature for the home relay in a D.C. line control circuit is

    A. KR
    B. H
    C. COS
    D. D

37. The nomenclature for the call-on relay is

    A. COS
    B. C
    C. CT
    D. CGD

38. The nomenclature for train stop is

    A. T
    B. S
    C. TS
    D. V

39. The nomenclature for a time element relay is

    A. U
    B. T
    C. S
    D. Q

40. The nomenclature for a track repeater relay is

    A. T
    B. TP
    C. TT
    D. TR

KEY (CORRECT ANSWERS)

1. A	11. B	21. C	31. B
2. C	12. B	22. B	32. B
3. D	13. B	23. B	33. A
4. D	14. C	24. B	34. A
5. B	15. A	25. C	35. D
6. B	16. D	26. B	36. B
7. B	17. B	27. A	37. A
8. A	18. C	28. A	38. D
9. C	19. D	29. D	39. A
10. D	20. C	30. B	40. B

EXAMINATION SECTION
TEST 1

DIRECTIONS: Each question or incomplete statement is followed by several suggested answers or completions. Select the one that BEST answers the question or completes the statement. *PRINT THE LETTER OF THE CORRECT ANSWER IN THE SPACE AT THE RIGHT.*

Questions 1-10.

DIRECTIONS: Questions 1 through 10 are for territory where A.C. line controls are used. Refer to the figure below when answering these questions.

The sketch below shows standard one-block-overlap control lines for automatic block signals. That is, each signal remains red while either of the two track circuits in advance is occupied, and each signal changes to green when the signal in advance becomes yellow.

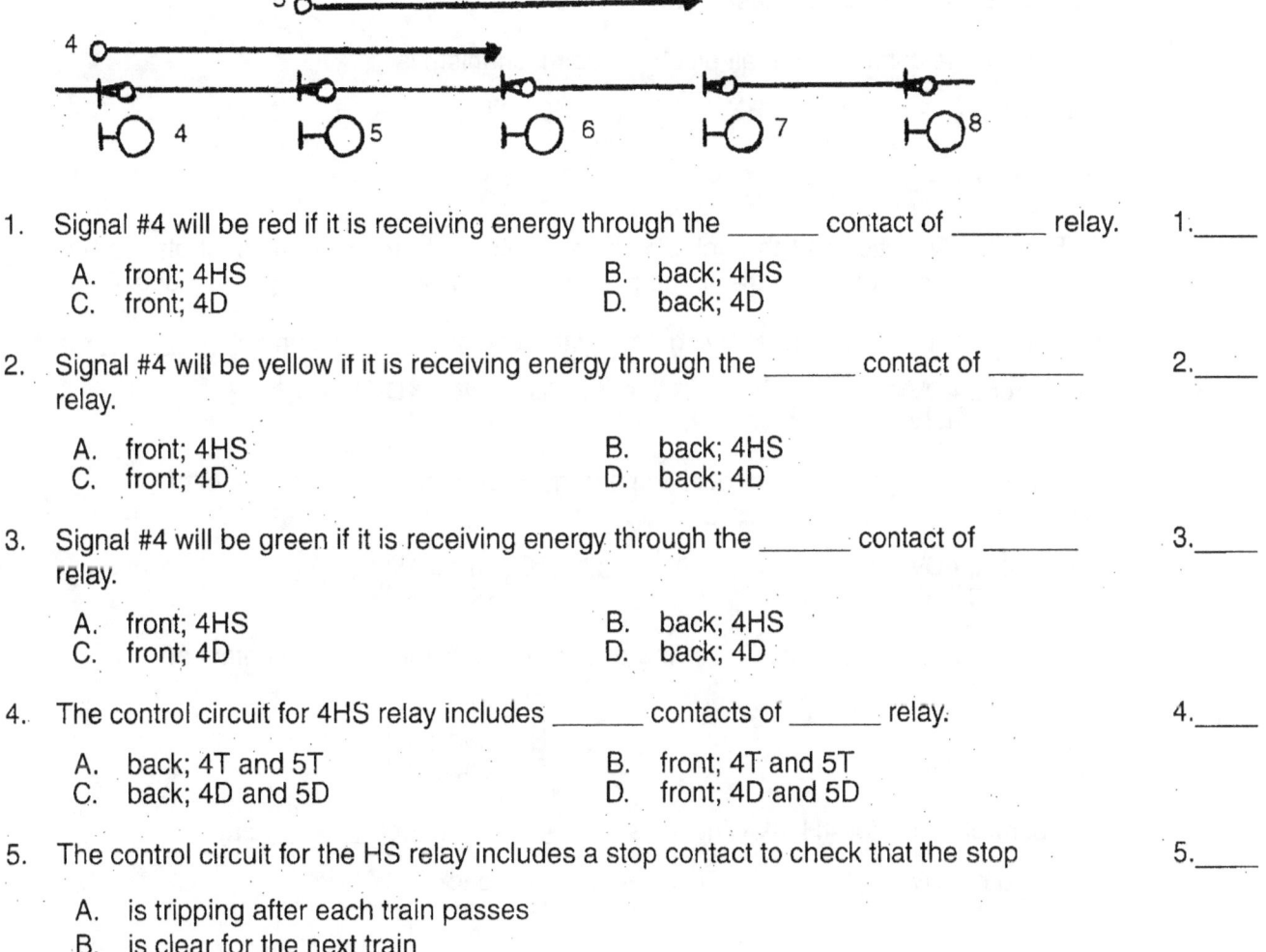

1. Signal #4 will be red if it is receiving energy through the _____ contact of _____ relay.   1._____

   A. front; 4HS
   B. back; 4HS
   C. front; 4D
   D. back; 4D

2. Signal #4 will be yellow if it is receiving energy through the _____ contact of _____ relay.   2._____

   A. front; 4HS
   B. back; 4HS
   C. front; 4D
   D. back; 4D

3. Signal #4 will be green if it is receiving energy through the _____ contact of _____ relay.   3._____

   A. front; 4HS
   B. back; 4HS
   C. front; 4D
   D. back; 4D

4. The control circuit for 4HS relay includes _____ contacts of _____ relay.   4._____

   A. back; 4T and 5T
   B. front; 4T and 5T
   C. back; 4D and 5D
   D. front; 4D and 5D

5. The control circuit for the HS relay includes a stop contact to check that the stop   5._____

   A. is tripping after each train passes
   B. is clear for the next train
   C. arm is not broken
   D. has received energy

57

6. In order to insure that the next signal is not red, the control circuit for 4D relay receives energy through a _____ contact in _____ relay.

   A. front; 4HS
   B. back; 4HS
   C. front; 5HS
   D. back; 5HS

7. Energy for the retaining control for the automatic stop associated with signal #4 is taken through a _____ contact in _____ relay.

   A. back; 4T
   B. front; 4T
   C. back; 4D
   D. front; 4D

8. A contact in the control circuit for 4D relay has the nomenclature

   A. 4VJ
   B. 4T
   C. 5T
   D. 5V

9. The stick circuit feature on the HS relay is necessary

   A. to insure that the HS relay will pick up properly
   B. to insure that the stop arm is clear
   C. to hold the HS relay picked up
   D. since it is not of the biased neutral type

10. Energy for the control of the all-electric stop mechanism is

    A. LB
    B. BX
    C. TB
    D. BH

Questions 11-20.

DIRECTIONS: Questions 11 through 20 are for territory where D.C. line controls are used. Refer to the figure on the previous page when answering these questions.

11. Signal #4 will be red if it is receiving energy through the _____ contact of _____ relay.

    A. front; 4DV
    B. back; 4DV
    C. front; 4HV
    D. back; 4HV

12. Signal #4 will be yellow if it is receiving energy through the _____ contact of _____ relay.

    A. front; 4DV
    B. back; 4DV
    C. front; 4HV
    D. back; 4HV

13. Signal #4 will be green if it is receiving energy through the _____ contact of _____ relay.

    A. front; 4DV
    B. back; 4DV
    C. front; 4HV
    D. back; 4HV

14. The control circuit for 4H relay includes a _____ contact of _____ relay.

    A. front; 4DV
    B. back; 4DV
    C. front; 4HV
    D. back; 4HV

15. In order to insure that the next signal is not red, the control circuit for 4DV relay receives energy through a front contact of _____ relay.

    A. 4T
    B. 5T
    C. 5HV
    D. 4H

16. The control circuit for 4HV relay includes a front contact of _____ relay. 16.____
    A. 4DV   B. 4T   C. 5T   D. 4H

17. The control circuit for 4DV relay is fed with _____ energy. 17.____
    A. LB & BX   B. BX & BH   C. LB & VB   D. BH & VB

18. The control circuit for 4HV relay includes a 18.____
    A. back contact of 4DV relay
    B. back contact of 4T relay
    C. stop contact
    D. back contact of 5T relay

19. If the distant relay for signal #4 is stuck in its deenergized position, the result will be that signal #4 will 19.____
    A. always display green   B. never display yellow
    C. never display green   D. be dark

20. Assume that signal #4 is green; signal #5 is yellow; and signal nos. 6, 7, and 8 are red. This condition would be brought about by a train on the track with its rear end 20.____
    A. between signal nos. 5 and 6
    B. between signal nos. 6 and 7
    C. between signal nos. 7 and 8
    D. past signal #8

21. Wire tags do NOT show the wire 21.____
    A. nomenclature   B. location
    C. size   D. destination

22. Safety considerations prohibit the use of carbon tetrachloride fire extinguishers on fires in the subway MAINLY because of the 22.____
    A. noxious fumes given off
    B. difficulty in refilling the extinguisher
    C. danger of damage to equipment
    D. shock hazard involved

23. The normal position of a switch lever on an all-electric conventional interlocking machine is 23.____
    A. pointing to the left   B. pointing to the right
    C. pushed all the way in   D. pulled all the way out

24. Standard flagging instructions require that the minimum distance a flagman is to place his portable trip and red lamp from the work area is 24.____
    A. 75 feet   B. 50 feet
    C. two car lengths   D. one-half car length

25. The emergency screw release on an interlocking machine is protected against unnecessary use by 25.____

A. an alarm that cannot be silenced
B. the control being in the trainmaster's office
C. a lead seal
D. a lock, with only the signal maintainer having a key

26. The distance from the gauge of rail to the side of the stop arm head nearest to the adjacent running rail is approximately

    A. 4" B. 5" C. 6" D. 7"

27. If a switch machine must be disconnected from the switch points, the FIRST person to be informed is the

    A. dispatcher B. supervisor, signals
    C. trainmaster D. towerman

28. One term that can properly be applied to the mechanical locking of a unit lever interlocking machine is

    A. apron B. bootleg C. dog D. frog

29. In accordance with standard practice, signal levers should be painted

    A. black B. white C. yellow D. red

30. In accordance with standard practice, switch levers should be painted

    A. yellow B. red C. black D. white

31. In accordance with standard practice, spare levers should be painted

    A. yellow B. black C. red D. white

32. One color of light NOT used to convey information at the latest type of pushbutton interlocking control panel is

    A. yellow B. white C. red D. blue

33. A 10 to 1 stepdown transformer has an input of 2 amperes at 110 volts. If losses are neglected, the maximum output of the transformer is _____ amperes at _____ volts.

    A. 2; 11 B. 20; 11 C. 2; 110 D. 20; 110

34. A signal maintainer need NOT inform his relief that

    A. the relief signal foreman is on duty
    B. the telephone is out of order
    C. single track operation is in effect
    D. the track section is renewing rails

35. One advantage of the double rail track circuit as compared to the single rail track circuit is that the double rail track circuit

    A. needs fewer insulated joints
    B. operates at a much lower current drain
    C. requires less equipment
    D. can be used for greater lengths of track circuit

36. The proper lantern signal to give a motorman to proceed past an out-of-service auto-   36._____
    matic signal in the subway is waving a

    A. white lantern across the track
    B. white lantern up and down
    C. green lantern across the track
    D. red lantern up and down

37. S.T. signals are generally used when it is desired to   37._____

    A. allow trains to *close-in* in approach to an occupied station
    B. limit speed of trains on a long downgrade
    C. reduce speed of trains on curves
    D. limit speed of trains through an interlocking

38. A signal maintainer would use a megger to test   38._____

    A. rail resistance   B. track voltage
    C. track current   D. insulation resistance

39. When connecting a track drill to operate from third rail power, the BEST practice is to   39._____
    connect to the

    A. negative rail then to the third rail
    B. third rail and then to the negative rail
    C. third rail and negative rail at same time
    D. signal rail then to the third rail

40. Whenever it is necessary to sectionalize a high tension signal main, a signal maintainer   40._____
    must

    A. de-energize both feeders at the same time
    B. first notify the trainmaster
    C. do exactly as instructed by supervision
    D. de-energize normal power before cutting-in reserve power

KEY (CORRECT ANSWERS)

1. B	11. D	21. C	31. A
2. D	12. B	22. A	32. D
3. C	13. A	23. C	33. B
4. B	14. A	24. A	34. A
5. A	15. C	25. C	35. D
6. C	16. D	26. B	36. B
7. A	17. C	27. B	37. A
8. D	18. C	28. C	38. D
9. C	19. C	29. D	39. A
10. B	20. C	30. C	40. C

TEST 2

DIRECTIONS: Each question or incomplete statement is followed by several suggested answers or completions. Select the one that BEST answers the question or completes the statement. *PRINT THE LETTER OF THE CORRECT ANSWER IN THE SPACE AT THE RIGHT.*

1. If a signal maintainer hooks down the automatic stop arm at a green automatic signal, the signal will

   A. change to yellow
   B. continue to display green
   C. become dark
   D. change to red

   1.____

2. According to official instructions, the outboard bearing of a train stop should be lubricated with

   A. zero oil as required
   B. light grease as required
   C. light grease monthly
   D. zero oil monthly

   2.____

3. Most signal heads are equipped with a means for determining the signal aspect from the rear of the signal. This device is called a

   A. distance repeater light
   B. stop repeater light
   C. flag arm repeater
   D. back light

   3.____

4. With the track circuit unoccupied, the voltage at the relay end of the track circuit will be

   A. higher at the relay terminals than at the rails
   B. exactly half the feed-end voltage
   C. lower than the voltage at the track transformer
   D. the same as the feed-end voltage

   4.____

5. If a test lamp lights when it is placed in series with a D.C. supply and a capacitor, the capacitor is PROBABLY

   A. open
   B. fully discharged
   C. shorted
   D. fully charged

   5.____

6. The amount of leakage current in a track circuit depends LEAST on the

   A. type of track construction
   B. extent of wear of the running rails
   C. condition of the ballast
   D. length of the track circuit

   6.____

7. One condition NOT likely to cause a track relay to be sluggish in picking up is a

   A. faulty insulated joint
   B. broken stop arm
   C. low feed-end voltage
   D. wet roadbed

   7.____

8. G.T. signals are GENERALLY used when it is desired to

   A. limit speed of trains through an interlocking
   B. limit speed of trains on a long downgrade
   C. reduce speed of trains on upgrade
   D. allow trains to *close-in* in approach to an occupied station

   8.____

9. The emergency screw release on an interlocking machine is protected against unnecessary use by

   A. an alarm that cannot be silenced
   B. the control being in the trainmaster's office
   C. a lead seal
   D. a lock, with only the signal maintainer having a key

10. The distance from the gauge of rail to the side of the stop arm head nearest to the adjacent running rail is APPROXIMATELY

    A. 4" B. 5" C. 6" D. 7"

11. If a switch machine must be disconnected from the switch points, the FIRST person to be informed is the

    A. dispatcher   B. supervisor, signals
    C. trainmaster   D. towerman

12. One term that can properly be applied to the mechanical locking of a unit lever interlocking machine is

    A. apron B. bootleg C. dog D. frog

13. In accordance with standard practice, signal levers should be painted

    A. black B. white C. yellow D. red

14. In accordance with standard practice, switch levers should be painted

    A. yellow B. red C. black D. white

15. In accordance with standard practice, spare levers should be painted

    A. yellow B. black C. red D. white

16. One color of light NOT used to convey information at the latest type of pushbutton interlocking control panel is

    A. yellow B. white C. red D. blue

17. A 10 to 1 stepdown transformer has an input of 2 amperes at 110 volts. If losses are neglected, the maximum output of the transformer is _____ amperes at _____ volts.

    A. 2; 11 B. 20; 11 C. 2; 110 D. 20; 110

Questions 18-27.

DIRECTIONS: Questions 18 through 27 are based on generally accepted transit system nomenclature.

18. The nomenclature for the normal switch correspondence relay is

    A. NWR B. NWC C. NWP D. NWZ

19. The nomenclature HY stands for home

    A. caution relay   B. relay (slotting)
    C. signal relay   D. yard relay

20. The letters used as a prefix for positive A.C. energy are 20.____
   A. BX   B. BH   C. LB   D. VB

21. The nomenclature for the distant control relay is 21.____
   A. DV   B. H   C. HS   D. COS

22. The nomenclature for the 14 volt D.C. line battery is 22.____
   A. LS   B. L   C. LE   D. LB

23. The nomenclature for the home relay in a D.C. line control circuit is 23.____
   A. KR   B. H   C. COS   D. D

24. The nomenclature for the call-on relay is 24.____
   A. COS   B. C   C. CT   D. CGD

25. The nomenclature for train stop is 25.____
   A. T   B. S   C. TS   D. V

26. The nomenclature for a time element relay, is 26.____
   A. U   B. T   C. S   D. Q

27. The nomenclature for a track repeater relay is 27.____
   A. T   B. TP   C. TT   D. TR

Questions 28-37.

DIRECTIONS: Questions 28 through 37 are for territory where A.C. line controls are used. Refer to the figure below when answering these questions.

The sketch below shows standard one-block-overlap control lines for automatic block signals. Assume signal equipment is operating properly unless otherwise stated

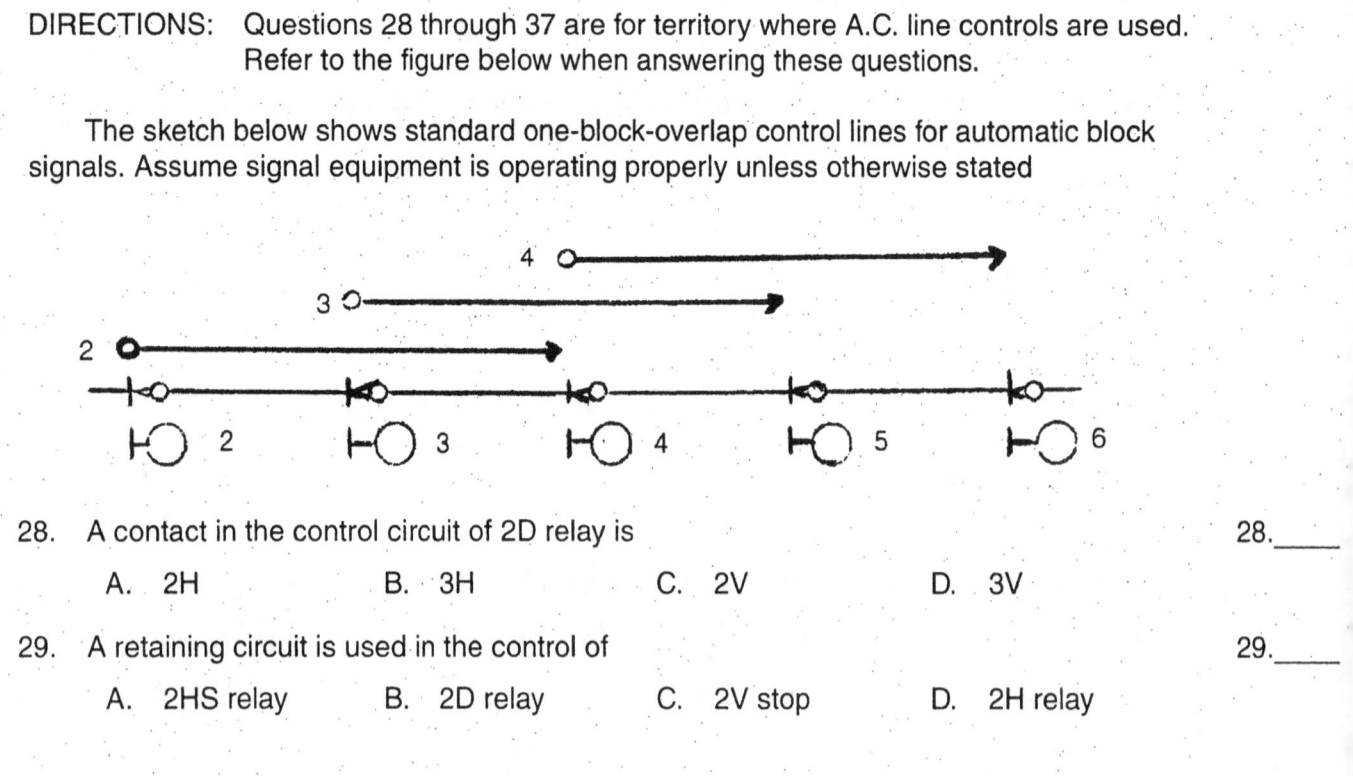

28. A contact in the control circuit of 2D relay is 28.____
   A. 2H   B. 3H   C. 2V   D. 3V

29. A retaining circuit is used in the control of 29.____
   A. 2HS relay   B. 2D relay   C. 2V stop   D. 2H relay

30. The energy supplied to the HS relay is

   A. BX　　　B. LB　　　C. BH　　　D. TB

31. A front contact in the control circuit of 2HS relay is

   A. 2T　　　B. 2H　　　C. 2D　　　D. 2VJ

32. A contact in the control circuit of 2D relay is

   A. 2HS　　　B. 3HS　　　C. -T　　　D. 3T

33. Once the HS relay is picked up, it stays energized even when the stop goes to the clear position by a

   A. track relay contact　　　B. stick feature
   C. stop contact　　　D. hold clear coil

34. Signal #3 displays a green aspect if it is receiving energy through a _____ contact of _____ relay.

   A. front; 3T　　　B. front; 3D
   C. back; 3HS　　　D. back; 3T

35. Signal #3 displays a yellow aspect if it 4.3 receiving energy through a _____ contact of _____ relay.

   A. front; 3D　　　B. front; 3T
   C. back; 3D　　　D. back; 3T

36. Signal #3 always displays a red aspect if the _____ relay is _____

   A. D; energized　　　B. D; de-energized
   C. HS; energized　　　D. HS; de-energized

37. When the rear of a train is between signals 5 and 6, the signal that is displaying a yellow aspect is signal number

   A. 2　　　B. 3　　　C. 4　　　D. 5

38. Water is NOT to be used to extinguish fires near the third rail. The MOST important reason is that water

   A. will cause harmful steam
   B. may transmit an electrical shock
   C. will make the track slippery
   D. may damage the third rail insulation

39. In an accident report, the information which is MOST useful in decreasing the recurrence of similar type accidents is the

   A. cause of the accident
   B. extent of injuries sustained
   C. time the accident happened
   D. number of people involved

40. When summoning an ambulance for an injured person, it is MOST important to give the 40.____
    A. name of the injured person
    B. cause of the accident
    C. location of the injured person
    D. nature of the injuries

KEY (CORRECT ANSWERS)

1. B	11. B	21. A	31. A
2. C	12. C	22. D	32. B
3. D	13. D	23. B	33. B
4. C	14. C	24. A	34. B
5. C	15. A	25. D	35. C
6. B	16. D	26. A	36. D
7. B	17. B	27. B	37. B
8. B	18. B	28. D	38. B
9. C	19. B	29. C	39. A
10. B	20. A	30. A	40. C

TEST 3

DIRECTIONS: Each question or incomplete statement is followed by several suggested answers or completions. Select the one that BEST answers the question or completes the statement. *PRINT THE LETTER OF THE CORRECT ANSWER IN THE SPACE AT THE RIGHT.*

Questions 1-10.

DIRECTIONS: Questions 1 through 10 are for territory where D.,C. line controls are used. Refer to the figure below when answering these questions.

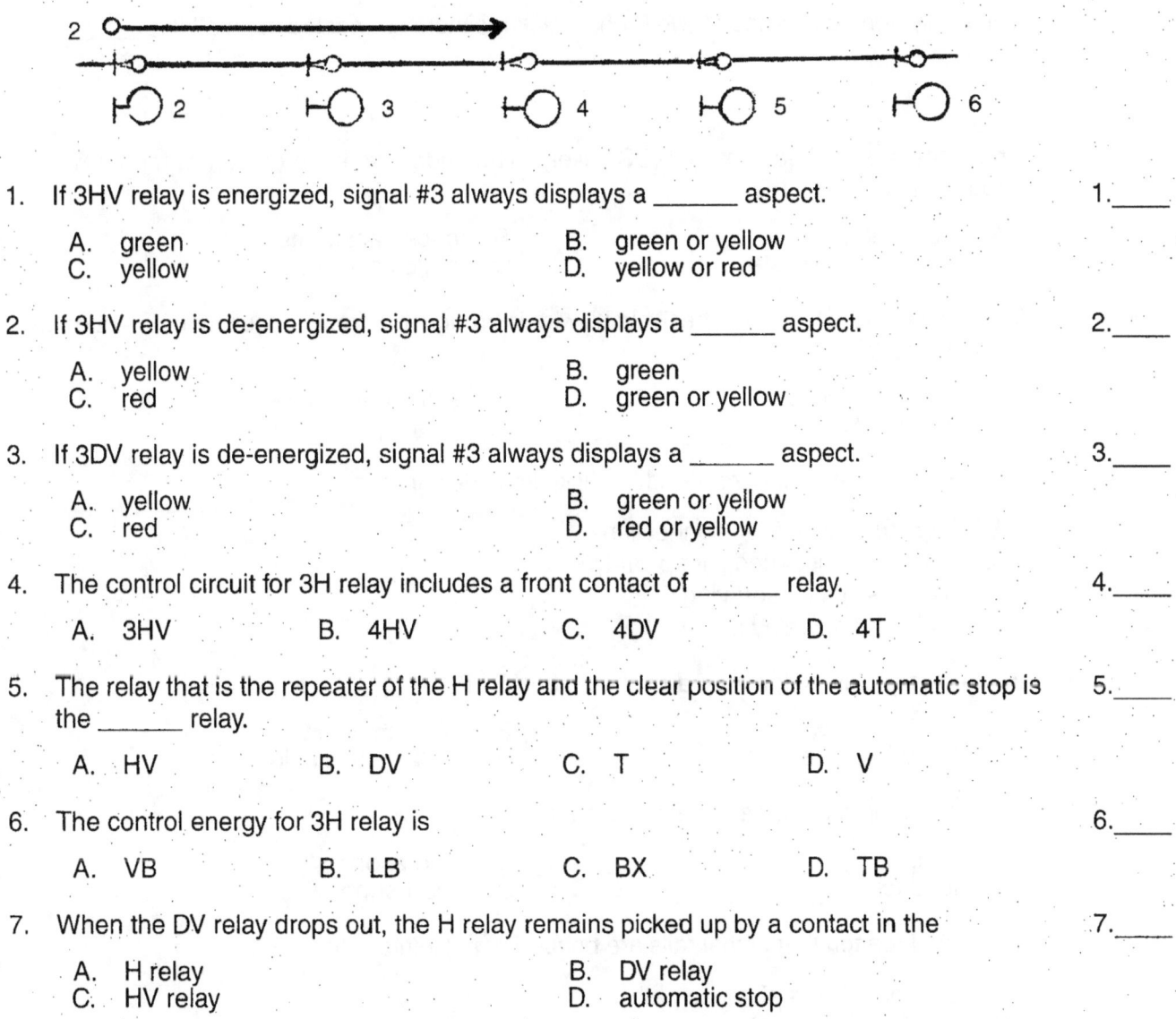

1. If 3HV relay is energized, signal #3 always displays a _____ aspect. 1.____

   A. green B. green or yellow
   C. yellow D. yellow or red

2. If 3HV relay is de-energized, signal #3 always displays a _____ aspect. 2.____

   A. yellow B. green
   C. red D. green or yellow

3. If 3DV relay is de-energized, signal #3 always displays a _____ aspect. 3.____

   A. yellow B. green or yellow
   C. red D. red or yellow

4. The control circuit for 3H relay includes a front contact of _____ relay. 4.____

   A. 3HV B. 4HV C. 4DV D. 4T

5. The relay that is the repeater of the H relay and the clear position of the automatic stop is the _____ relay. 5.____

   A. HV B. DV C. T D. V

6. The control energy for 3H relay is 6.____

   A. VB B. LB C. BX D. TB

7. When the DV relay drops out, the H relay remains picked up by a contact in the 7.____

   A. H relay B. DV relay
   C. HV relay D. automatic stop

8. The control energy for 3HV relay is 8.____

   A. VB B. LB C. BX D. TB

67

9. The control circuit for 3V all-electric stop includes a _____ contact of _____ relay.

   A. front; 3H
   B. back; 3HV
   C. front; 3HV
   D. front; 3T

10. The control circuit of 3DV relay includes front and back contacts of _____ relay.

    A. 3HV
    B. 4HV
    C. 3H
    D. 3T

11. The MOST important reason for blocking out dust and moisture from subway signal cases is to prevent

    A. corrosion of contacts and wires
    B. decay of prints
    C. unnecessary painting
    D. unsanitary working conditions

12. The equivalent resistance of two 6-ohm track resistors connected in parallel is _____ ohms.

    A. 12
    B. 6
    C. 3
    D. 1.5

13. The piece of signal equipment MOST likely to be under water if a broken water main floods the subway is the

    A. track relay
    B. track transformer
    C. track repeater relay
    D. switch circuit controller

14. The device through which a track circuit wire is brought out from conduit for connection to the rail is called the

    A. signal rail bond
    B. shunt rail adapter
    C. S connector
    D. bootleg

15. One fail-safe feature incorporated in track circuit design is

    A. high current bootleg connections
    B. staggered insulated joint polarity
    C. high resistance shunting
    D. multi-contact relays

16. In the clear position, the stop arm should be AT LEAST _____ top of rail.

    A. 1/2 inch above
    B. 1/2 inch below
    C. 2 1/2 inches above
    D. 2 1/2 inches below

17. The whistle or horn signal for a signal maintainer is

    A. short-long
    B. long-short
    C. long-long
    D. short-short

18. The MAIN reason that signal rails are bonded at rail joints is to

    A. provide a low resistance path
    B. provide a high resistance path
    C. reduce ballast resistance
    D. replace impedance bonds

19. A manipulation chart is used to determine the 19.____

    A. proper operating procedure for car equipment
    B. correct sequence of cars to be sent into the yard
    C. correct combination of levers for a route
    D. schedule of intervals at a gap point

20. On unit-lever interlocking machines, signal maintainers are usually NOT permitted to disconnect the mechanical locking from a switch lever because 20.____

    A. this cannot be done easily by one man alone
    B. this will prevent other levers from operating
    C. this will damage the lever guide
    D. part of the safety features of the interlocking will be defeated

21. According to the rules, a signal maintainer may operate an interlocking plant in an emergency provided that he 21.____

    A. is ordered to do so by the dispatcher
    B. receives permission from the office of the supervisor of signals
    C. has worked the interlocking regularly
    D. has been qualified by the towerman

22. One dangerous condition that can arise in a 4-track subway area with single rail track circuits is that 22.____

    A. bonding of rails will cause excessive propulsion current to flow in the signal rail
    B. removal of a negative rail may not cause any track relay to drop
    C. breakdown of two consecutive insulated joints will prevent proper shunting of track circuits
    D. the signal will always stay green if the stop arm is hooked down

23. The instrument that should be used to check the setting of time relays is a _____ timer. 23.____

    A. reset   B. synchronous
    C. gap   D. solenoid

24. According to standard instructions, the shunting sensitivity of track circuits should be checked 24.____

    A. semi-annually   B. quarterly
    C. monthly   D. annually

25. A signal maintainer, when checking the fouling adjustment of a switch movement, should place the obstruction gage 25.____

    A. 6 inches from the tip of the point
    B. at tip of the point
    C. 3 1/2 inches from the tip of the point
    D. opposite the basket rod

26. Signal maintainers are always cautioned to check on the location of trains before adjusting or servicing any signal equipment PRIMARILY to prevent 26.____

    A. electrical shock   B. wrong routing of a train
    C. damage to signal equipment D. tripping of a train

27. A signal maintainer need NOT inform his relief that

   A. the relief signal foreman is on duty
   B. the telephone is out of order
   C. single track operation is in effect
   D. the track section is renewing rails

28. One advantage of the double rail track circuit as compared to the single rail track circuit is that the double rail track circuit

   A. needs fewer insulated joints
   B. operates at a much lower current drain
   C. requires less equipment
   D. can be used for greater lengths of track circuit

29. The proper lantern signal to give a motorman to proceed past an out-of-service automatic signal in the subway is waving a

   A. white lantern across the track
   B. white lantern up and down
   C. green lantern across the track
   D. red lantern up and down

30. S.T. signals are GENERALLY used when it is desired to

   A. allow trains to *close-in* in approach to an occupied station
   B. limit speed of trains on a long downgrade
   C. reduce speed of trains on curves
   D. limit speed of trains through an interlocking

31. A signal maintainer would use a megger to test

   A. rail resistance   B. track voltage
   C. track current   D. insulation resistance

32. When connecting a track drill to operate from third rail power, the BEST practice is to connect to the

   A. negative rail then to the third rail
   B. third rail then to the negative rail
   C. third rail and negative rail at the same time
   D. signal rail then to the third rail

33. Whenever it is necessary to sectionalize a high tension signal main, a signal maintainer must

   A. de-energize both feeders at the same time
   B. first notify the trainmaster
   C. do exactly as instructed by supervision
   D. de-energize normal power before cutting-in reserve power

Questions 34-38.

DIRECTIONS: Questions 34 through 38 are based on the system of signal indications that is used.

34. An interlocking signal indicating *proceed with caution prepared to stop within vision, expecting to find track occupied* displays a _____ aspect.

    A. green over yellow
    B. yellow
    C. green
    D. green over green

35. An interlocking signal indicating *proceed on diverging route* displays a _____ aspect.

    A. green over yellow
    B. yellow over green
    C. green
    D. yellow

36. An automatic signal indicating *proceed prepared to stop at next signal* displays a _____ aspect.

    A. green over green
    B. green over yellow
    C. red
    D. yellow

37. An interlocking signal indicating *proceed on main route* displays a _____ aspect.

    A. green over yellow
    B. green over green
    C. yellow over yellow
    D. yellow over green

38. The letter among the following which is NOT usually connected with time-controlled signals is

    A. T   B. GT   C. S   D. P

39. Wire tags do NOT show the wire

    A. nomenclature
    B. location
    C. size
    D. destination

40. Standard flagging instructions require that the minimum distance a flagman is to place his portable trip and red lamp from the work area is

    A. 75 feet
    B. 50 feet
    C. two car lengths
    D. one-half car length

KEY (CORRECT ANSWERS)

1. B	11. A	21. B	31. D
2. C	12. C	22. B	32. A
3. D	13. D	23. B	33. C
4. D	14. D	24. C	34. B
5. A	15. B	25. A	35. A
6. B	16. B	26. D	36. D
7. A	17. B	27. A	37. B
8. A	18. A	28. D	38. D
9. A	19. C	29. B	39. C
10. A	20. D	30. A	40. A

EXAMINATION SECTION
TEST 1

DIRECTIONS: Each question or incomplete statement is followed by several suggested answers or completions. Select the one that BEST answer the question or completes the statement. *PRINT THE LETTER OF THE CORRECT ANSWER IN THE SPACE AT THE RIGHT.*

1. Signal power transformers installed in the subway are elevated above the floor. The reason for elevating these transformers is to 1.____

    A. allow free air circulation for cooling
    B. decrease the likelihood of submersion in a flood
    C. permit easy draining of the oil from the case
    D. make the leads more accessible for maintenance

2. As a signal maintainer, one of the BEST ways of cooperating with your foreman would be to 2.____

    A. bring to his attention any infraction of the rules committed by others
    B. discuss with him all the details of the work assigned to you
    C. accept the responsibility of the work assigned to you
    D. try to improve the signal system by frequently suggesting circuit changes

3. The negative rails on most of the subway system are cross-bonded at frequent intervals. One *disadvantage* that results from this practice is that 3.____

    A. the tracing of signal circuits is made more difficult
    B. some broken rail protection is lost
    C. track circuits are: more complicated
    D. the signal apparatus must carry more d.c.

4. A signal maintainer about to give a "proceed" hand signal at a home signal indicating "stop" should NOT give the hand signal until he is sure that all switches in the route are properly set, and until the 4.____

    A. proper lamps or flags have been set out
    B. a train dispatcher has been notified
    C. motorman has stopped the train
    D. motorman sounds four blasts of the whistle

5. If a track circuit at an interlocking fails to operate when its transformer and resistor adjustments are the same as on similar track circuits, the one of the following conditions which could NOT be responsible is 5.____

    A. open switch indication contacts
    B. loose connections to the transformer
    C. poor bonding of either rail
    D. broken switch rod insulation

6. A signal maintainer testing for opposite polarities on two adjacent unoccupied track circuits bridges the insulated joint separating the two circuits. If the polarities are opposite, a *green* signal at the bridged joint will generally 6.____

A. remain green and the automatic stop will stay down
B. go red and the automatic stop will stay down
C. remain green and the automatic stop will go up
D. go red and the automatic stop will go up

7. The condition which would LEAST likely cause a feed-end fuse on a single-rail track circuit to blow is a

   A. train standing on the circuit too long
   B. number of lamp banks and tools connected to the third rail and the signal rail
   C. short circuit between third rail and signal rail due to dragging equipment
   D. short circuited feed-end track resistor

8. A certain signal will clear if approached at a speed of 35 m.p.h.
   If the track circuit in the approach to this signal is 650 ft. long and the automatic stop clears in about 2 seconds, the time relay setting should be *approximately*

   A. 11 seconds   B. 13 seconds   C. 15 seconds   D. 17 seconds

9. At an automatic signal location, the device having NONE of its contacts included in the signal lighting circuit is the

   A. automatic stop   B. track relay
   C. distant relay   D. home relay

10. When signal rail bonds are installed they must be driven into the rail IMMEDIATELY after the rail has been drilled.
    The logical reason for this requirement is

    A. to get the connection made before the hole rusts
    B. to minimize the danger of damaging the bond terminal
    C. that the heat of drilling has expanded the hole
    D. that they must be in place before the fish plates are installed

11. When standing on the signal platform testing circuits in a signal case on the elevated structure on a rainy day, the maintainer should be especially cautious *mainly* because

    A. the platform is likely to be charged
    B. leakage current from the third rail may be very high
    C. wet hands and equipment increase the probability of shock
    D. the signal case may not be grounded

12. All seals on an interlocking machine MUST be inspected daily by the signal maintainer, and any broken seals reported at once to the office of the

    A. dispatcher   B. trainmaster
    C. supervisor   D. signal foreman

13. The MINIMUM time setting of mechanical time releases on signal levers is required by official instructions to be

    A. 15 seconds   B. 20 seconds   C. 25 seconds   D. 30 seconds

14. If the signal maintainer hooks down the stop arm at a home signal which is displaying red over red, the signal will   14.____

    A. clear
    B. become dark
    C. change its indication to a call-on
    D. continue to display red over red

15. When a lever is moved to reverse a switch, the actual locking of conflicting levers takes place while the lever is being moved from   15.____

    A. normal to normal indication
    B. normal indication to center
    C. center to reverse indication
    D. reverse indication to reverse

16. One difference between a double-rail track circuit and a single-rail track circuit is that, in a double-rail track circuit, both running rails   16.____

    A. carry signal current   B. are grounded
    C. have insulated joints   D. have guard rails

17. The handle of a spare lever in an interlocking machine should be painted   17.____

    A. black   B. red   C. blue   D. yellow

18. After a train moves off a track circuit, the signal maintainer notices that the track relay picks up slowly.
    This sluggish pick up *could* be due to   18.____

    A. reversal of local element connections
    B. a developing fault at the insulated joint
    C. high track circuit voltage
    D. having more front contacts than back contacts

19. G.T. signals are *generally* used when it is desirable to limit the speed of trains   19.____

    A. approaching occupied passenger stations
    B. on long down grades
    C. through main line interlockings
    D. while skipping regular passenger stations

20. If an a.c. ammeter is connected across the feed-end resistor terminals of a track circuit with the feed-end fuse removed, the ammeter will   20.____

    A. burn out
    B. indicate zero current
    C. read the total current of the track circuit
    D. measure track leakage current *only*

21. A signal maintainer knows he is the one being called when he hears   21.____

    A. four short whistle blasts
    B. two long followed by two short whistle blasts

C. one long followed by one short whistle blast
D. three short whistle blasts

22. The track circuit condition which will, in general, require the LOWEST voltage for successful operation is a

   A. short dry section
   B. short wet section
   C. long dry section
   D. long wet section

23. In counting the number of plates of a full-wave copper-oxide rectifier used on the signal system, you would know that there was an error if the number counted was

   A. 16   B. 20   C. 30   D. 36

QUESTIONS 24-31.
Questions 24 to 31 inclusive are based on the wiring diagram shown below.

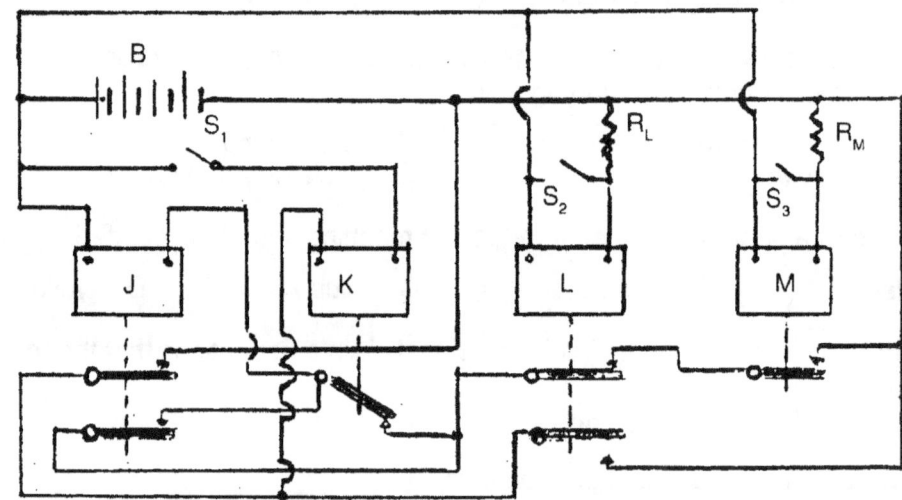

NOTE: In the above diagram, devices J, K, L, and M are relays which function properly in the circuits shown; S_1, S_2, and S_3 are switches; R_L and R_M, are resistors; B is a battery.

Each question in Column I below gives a combination of the positions of switches S_1, S_2, and S_3. Each combination in Column I will result in energizing one of the combinations of relays shown in Column II. For each combination of switch positions in Column I, select the resulting combination of energized relays from Column II.

COLUMN I
(switch positions)

	S_1	S_2	S_3
24.	open	open	open
25.	closed	open	open
26.	open	open	closed
27.	open	closed	closed
28.	open	closed	open
29.	closed	closed	open
30.	closed	open	closed
31.	closed	closed	closed

COLUMN II
(energized relays)

A. none
B. J
C. K
D. L
E. M
H. K and M
O. K, L, and M
P. J, L, and M
S. J, K, and L
T. All

32. In a properly operating automatic signal lighting circuit, when a distant relay is deenergized the signal will display

    A. red
    B. yellow
    C. green or yellow depending on the position of the home relay
    D. red or yellow depending on the position of the home relay

33. A lever time release is *generally* used to shunt out contacts on a

    A. lock relay
    B. detector relay
    C. switch indicating relay
    D. approach track relay

34. When a 1:2:4 mix of concrete is specified, it means

    A. 1 part sand, 2 parts broken stone, and 4 parts cement
    B. 1 part cement, 2 parts sand, and 4 parts broken stone
    C. 1 part cement, 2 parts broken stone, and 4 parts sand
    D. 1 part sand, 2 parts cement, and 4 parts broken stone

35. If a test lamp lights when placed in series with a condenser and a suitable source of d.c., it is a *good* indication that the condenser is

    A. fully charged
    B. short-circuited
    C. fully discharged
    D. open-circuited

36. If two 2.4-ohm track resistors are connected in parallel, the resulting resistance will be _____ ohms.

    A. 0.41
    B. 0.6
    C. 1.2
    D. 4.8

37. A *satisfactory* test to determine whether the locknuts in a terminal box have loosened is to

    A. tap the nuts with an insulating handle
    B. try to loosen the nuts with a pair of pliers
    C. jiggle the wires at their terminals
    D. try to tighten the nuts with a socket wrench

38. When a signal maintainer cuts out a circuit, he must make a record of this occurence. It is NOT necessary to include in this record the

    A. reason for cutting out the circuit
    B. name of the circuit
    C. time that the circuit was cut out and the time restored to normal
    D. name and number of the towerman on duty

39. When it is necessary for both you and your helper to perform routine maintenance work on a stop mechanism which is located between the running rails on straight level track in the subway, a *prime* safety precaution is to

    A. place a red lantern between the rails about 50 feet away
    B. work so that you and your helper face oncoming traffic
    C. notify the trainmaster before starting work
    D. request a flagman to cover this work

40. If a section of the subway became flooded with water to a depth of about 4 inches above the base of the running rails, one *positive* effect on the signal system would be that a number of

    A. track fuses would blow out
    B. track feed resistors would burn out
    C. fibre insulated joints would be damaged
    D. track relays would be dropped out

KEY (CORRECT ANSWERS)

1.	B	11.	C	21.	C	31.	C
2.	C	12.	C	22.	A	32.	D
3.	B	13.	B	23.	C	33.	D
4.	C	14.	D	24.	P	34.	B
5.	A	15.	A	25.	T	35.	B
6.	B	16.	C	26.	D	36.	C
7.	A	17.	D	27.	A	37.	D
8.	A	18.	B	28.	E	38.	D
9.	B	19.	B	29.	H	39.	B
10.	A	20.	B	30.	D	40.	D

TEST 2

DIRECTIONS: Each question or incomplete statement is followed by several suggested answers or completions. Select the one that BEST answers the questions or completes the statement. *PRINT THE LETTER OF THE CORRECT ANSWER IN SPACE AT THE RIGHT.*

1. If in doubt as to the meaning of any rule, regulation, or instruction, the BEST procedure for a maintainer to follow is to

    A. obtain an explanation from his union delegate
    B. obtain an explanation from another maintainer
    C. use his best judgment when a situation arises
    D. obtain an explanation from the foreman

    1.____

2. In flagging down a train with a regulation maintainer's lantern, the lantern should be

    A. moved violently above the head
    B. swung back and forth across the track
    C. moved rapidly up and down
    D. swung in a vertical circle at arm's length

    2.____

3. A maintainer making the regular rounds of his section finds that one of the two yellow lanterns hanging at a particular location alongside the track is dark.
His BEST action would be to

    A. operate the nearest emergency alarm
    B. notify the trainmaster
    C. tell the flagman
    D. remain there and flag the next train

    3.____

4. When it is necessary for both you and your helper to perform routine maintenance work on a stop mechanism which is located between the running rails in the subway, a *prime* safety precaution is to

    A. place a red lantern between the rails about 50 feet away
    B. work so that you and your helper face oncoming traffic
    C. request a flagman to cover this work
    D. notify the trainmaster before starting work

    4.____

5. When a maintainer finds it necessary to operate an emergency alarm because he sees dense smoke in the subway, the FIRST action he should take after pulling the lever is to

    A. call the trainmaster to report his finding
    B. take the nearest fire extinguisher and look for the fumes
    C. notify his foreman
    D. warn passengers so as to avoid panic

    5.____

6. When men are working on the track a short distance beyond the leaving end of a station, the flagman should place the warning yellow lanterns

    A. about 500 feet in the approach to the station
    B. at both ends of the station
    C. about the center of the station
    D. at the last car stop marker

    6.____

7. At an automatic signal location, the device having NONE of its contacts included in the signal lighting circuit is the

   A. automatic stop
   B. track relay
   C. distant relay
   D. home relay

8. Track switches that are in regular daily operation should be inspected

   A. daily
   B. weekly
   C. every two weeks
   D. monthly

9. A switch machine must be so adjusted that it will not lock up when an obstruction test gauge is properly placed between either switch point and the stock rail. The thickness of this obstruction test gauge is

   A. 3/32 inch   B. 3/16 inch   C. 3/8 inch   D. 3/4 inch

10. A reason for making the adjustment in the preceding question is to

    A. standardize the flangeway at turnouts
    B. check that the stock rail is properly offset at the point of switch
    C. hold signal levers mechanically locked if the switch movement is incomplete
    D. insure that signal indications agree with the position of the switch

11. A transit employee is required by the rules to make a written report on even the most minor unjury to himself. A *good* reason for having this requirement is that

    A. employees will be careful to avoid injury because they dislike making out reports
    B. it is one of the rules of the transit system
    C. in case of a serious injury, the employee will remember how to fill out a proper report
    D. the employee is not the best judge of the seriousness of an injury

12. Of the following, it is LEAST important for a maintainer to inform his relief that a

    A. section of signal rail including a switch is grounded
    B. new towerman has been assigned to their section
    C. signal in their section has been reported as having a cracked green lens
    D. new bulletin has been issued covering the maintenance of switch machines

13. The maintainer in a yard should be especially cautious when testing circuits in signal cases on a rainy day *mainly* because

    A. rails are slippery, so accidental tripping of trains must be particularly avoided
    B. leakage due to the rain may give erroneous test results
    C. wet hands and test equipment increase the probability of shock
    D. Do signal cases are likely to be grounded by the rain

14. The leakage current of a track circuit can be measured by connecting an a.c. ammeter to the

    A. feed fuse clips with both relay and feed fuses removed
    B. relay fuse clips with only the relay fuse removed
    C. rails with both relay and feed fuses removed
    D. rails with only the relay fuse removed

15. If a signal maintainer in the subway hears a train whistle he would know that he is the person wanted if he hears   15.____

    A. two short blasts
    B. two long blasts
    C. a short blast followed by a long one
    D. a long blast followed by a short one

QUESTIONS 16-25.

Questions 16 to 25 inclusive in Column I are the names or operating conditions of signal or associated track equipment, each of which is represented by the three symbols next to one of the letters in Column II. For each question in Column I, select the representative symbol from Column II. PRINT on your answer sheet, in the correspondingly numbered item space, the letter given beside your selected symbol.

COLUMN I
(equipment or operating condition)

16. Lever latch contact
17. Home relay contact which completes the circuit to the red light
18. Track switch which is set for turnout move when its controlling lever is normal
19. Track relay contact used in automatic stop retaining circuit
20. Time relay
21. Front contact on distant relay
22. Push button which breaks circuit when operated
23. Automatic stop contact which is closed when the stop is clear
24. Back contact on home relay
25. Relay which is used to select between the yellow and green lights

26. The sketches at the right show the ends of two 12-conductor signal control cables that are to be spliced. If conductors 6 and L are the FIRST to be connected, then it is correct to connect conductors
    A. 12 and I
    B. 12 and G
    C. 10 and G
    D. 10 and H

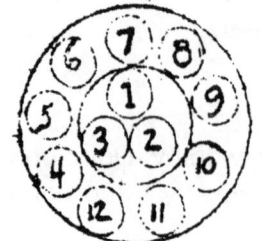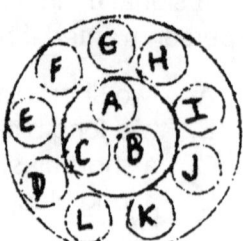

27. The resistor at the right has two intermediate taps and is connected in a circuit as indicated. The effect of the two cross connections shown is to
    A. short-circuit sections 1 and 3, leaving section 2 alone in the circuit
    B. parallel sections 2 and 3, and place them in series with section 1
    C. connect all three sections in parallel with one another
    D. place the series combination of sections 2 and 3 in parallel with section 1

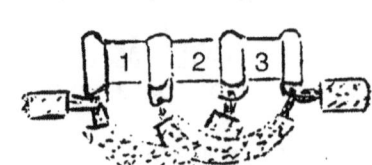

QUESTIONS 28-34.
Question 28 to 34 inclusive are based on the sketch below showing a series of automatic signals along an express track in the subway. All signals have standard one-block-overlap home controls, and there are no time controls or overlapped distant controls: That is, each signal remains red while either of the two track circuits in advance is occupied, and each signal changes to green when the signal in advance becomes yellow. The arrangement of equipment in the signal cases at each signal location is standard. The track is to be assumed clear of trains unless otherwise stated in an item. Refer to this sketch in answering these questions.

Direction of Traffic

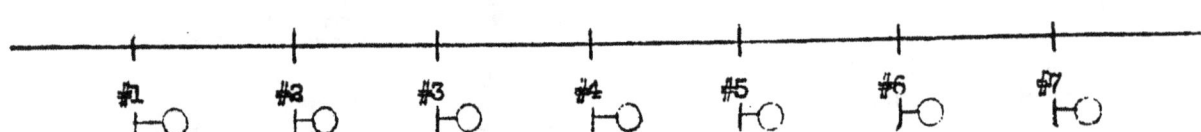

28. The numbers of all the signals which would NOT display green as a consequence of an insulated joint breakdown at signal #4 are

    A. 1, 2, 3, and 4   B. 2, 3, and 4
    C. 3, 4, and 5   D. 2, 3, 4, and 5

29. If the track feed fuse at the defective insulated joint in question 28 is removed, the result in *most* cases will be that

    A. the track relay at signal #3 will pick up
    B. signal #3 will become yellow and signal #2 green
    C. signal #4 will become green and the other affected signals will not change
    D. conditions will remain unchanged

30. The removal of the relay fuse instead of the track feed fuse in question 29 would *generally* result in

    A. picking up of the track relay at signal #3
    B. signal #3 becoming yellow and signal #2 green
    C. signal #4 becoming green without change in the other signals
    D. no change in conditions

31. If signal #3 is yellow, signal #4 is red with its automatic stop in the trip position, and the remaining signals are green, the cause of this condition could be a

    A. blown track fuse at signal #4
    B. open wire in the home control of signal #4
    C. open wire in the distant control of signal #4
    D. open wire in the stop retaining circuit of signal #4

32. If a break occurs in the stop clearing circuit of signal #5, the number of signals that will display yellow as a result is

    A. 0   B. 1   C. 2   D. 3

33. Assume that a long train has stopped with its front end a car-length past signal #5, and its rear end between signals nos. 3 and 4, although signal #6 is clear.
    Under these conditions, the number of automatic stops retained clear by the train is

    A. 2   B. 3   C. 4   D. 5

34. Under the conditions in question 33, the number of signals I displaying red is

    A. 2   B. 3   C. 4   D. 5

35. A switch should NOT be operated by means of the emergency release unless the

    A. controlling signal lever has first been reversed
    B. normal source of power fails
    C. switch lever is locked in the normal position
    D. track section including the switch is unoccupied

36. A maintainer and helper on the day trick are walking along a local track of a four-track subway line when the helper trips and strikes his head on one of the running rails.
    The maintainer is NOT strong enough to move the unconscious man alone.
    The BEST of the following actions for the maintainer to take is to

    A. walk toward the next train and flag it down
    B. proceed to the nearest telephone and call assistance
    C. try to revive the helper and get him on to the bench walk
    D. shunt the track circuit to trip any approaching train

37. Of the following, the *most likely* cause of blown track fuses in a yard track circuit is a

    A. defective switch heater
    B. grounded negative rail
    C. short-circuited insulated joint
    D. broken signal rail bond

38. A condition which could result in slow drop-away of a track relay when a train enters the track circuit is

   A. insulated joint fouled with steel dust
   B. bootleg connections fouled with water
   C. track feed resistor set too high
   D. track feed voltage adjusted too high

38.____

39. It is standard practice to use 40 feet of #14 wire as the equivalent of a 0.1-ohm resistor in checking the shunting sensitivity of track circuits.
From this, it can be reasoned that the resistance of a 1,000-foot coil of #14 wire is about

   A. 0.25 ohms   B. 1.25 ohms   C. 2.5 ohms   D. 12.5 ohms

39.____

40. If a maintainer finds that it is necessary to hook down the stop arm at an automatic signal, he MUST

   A. station his helper at that location until a regular flagman can be obtained
   B. hang a red warning lantern on the signal
   C. first obtain permission
   D. notify the section dispatcher

40.____

KEY (CORRECT ANSWERS)

1.	D	11.	D	21.	K	31.	B
2.	B	12.	B	22.	E	32.	B
3.	C	13.	C	23.	B	33.	B
4.	B	14.	A	24.	W	34.	C
5.	A	15.	D	25.	M	35.	D
6.	B	16.	C	26.	D	36.	A
7.	B	17.	W	27.	C	37.	A
8.	A	18.	J	28.	A	38.	D
9.	B	19.	T	29.	C	39.	C
10.	C	20.	P	30.	D	40.	D

EXAMINATION SECTION
TEST 1

DIRECTIONS: Each question or incomplete statement is followed by several suggested answers or completions. Select the one that BEST answers the question or completes the statement. *PRINT THE LETTER OF THE CORRECT ANSWER IN THE SPACE AT THE RIGHT.*

1. The MOST important reason for blocking out dust and moisture from subway signal cases is to prevent

    A. corrosion of contacts and wires
    B. decay of prints
    C. unnecessary painting
    D. unsanitary working conditions

2. The equivalent resistance of two 6-ohm track resistors connected in parallel is _____ ohms.

    A. 12 B. 6 C. 3 D. 1.5

3. The piece of signal equipment *most likely* to be under water if a broken water main floods the subway is the

    A. track relay
    B. track transformer
    C. track repeater relay
    D. switch circuit controller

4. The device through which a track circuit wire is brought out from conduit for connection to the rail is called the

    A. signal rail bond
    B. shunt rail adapter
    C. S connector
    D. bootleg

5. One fail-safe feature incorporated in track circuit design is

    A. high current bootleg connections
    B. staggered insulated joint polarity
    C. high resistance shunting
    D. multi-contact relays

6. In the *clear* position, the stop arm should be at LEAST

    A. 1/2 inch above top of rail
    B. 1 1/2 inch below top of rail
    C. 2 1/2 inches above top of rail
    D. 2 1/2 inches below top of rail

7. The whistle or horn signal for a signal maintainer is

    A. short-long B. long-short C. long-long D. short-short

8. The MAIN reason that signal rails are bonded at rail joints is to

    A. provide a low resistance path
    B. provide a high resistance path
    C. reduce ballast resistance
    D. replace impedance bonds

9. A manipulation chart is used to determine the

   A. proper operating procedure for car equipment
   B. correct sequence of cars to be sent into the yard
   C. correct combination of levers for a route
   D. schedule of intervals at a gap point

10. On unit-lever interlocking machines, signal maintainers are usually NOT permitted to disconnect the mechanical locking from a switch lever because

    A. this cannot be done easily by one man alone
    B. this will prevent other levers from operating
    C. this will damage the lever guide
    D. part of the safety features of the interlocking will be defeated

11. According to the rules, a signal maintainer may operate an interlocking plant in an emergency provided that he

    A. is ordered to do so by the dispatcher
    B. receives permission from the office of the supervisor of signals
    C. has worked the interlocking regularly
    D. has been qualified by the towerman

12. One dangerous condition that can arise in a 4-track subway area with single rail track circuits is that

    A. bonding of rails will cause excessive propulsion current to flow in the single rail
    B. removal of a negative rail may not cause any track relay to drop
    C. breakdown of two consecutive insulated joints will prevent proper shunting of track circuits
    D. the signal will always stay green if the stop arm is hooked down

13. The instrument that should be used to check the setting of time relays is a _____ timer.

    A. reset   B. synchronous
    C. gap   D. selenoid

14. According to standard instructions, the shunting sensitivity of track circuits should be checked

    A. semi-annually B. quarterly
    C. monthly   D. annually

15. A signal maintainer, when checking the fouling adjustment of a switch movement, should place the obstruction gage

    A. 6" from the tip of the point
    B. at the tip of the point
    C. 3 1/2 inches from the tip
    D. opposite the basket rod

16. Signal maintainers are ALWAYS cautioned to check on the location of trains before adjusting or servicing any signal equipment primarily to prevent

    A. electrical shock   B. wrong routing of a train
    C. damage to signal equipment   D. tripping of a train

17. If a signal maintainer hooks down the automatic stop arm at a green automatic signal, the signal will

    A. change to yellow
    B. continue to display green
    C. become dark
    D. change to red

18. According to official instructions, the outboard bearing of a train stop should be lubricated with

    A. zero oil as required
    B. light grease as required
    C. light grease monthly
    D. zero oil monthly

19. Most signal heads are equipped with a means for determining the signal aspect from the rear of the signal.
    This device is called a

    A. distance light repeater
    B. stop repeater light
    C. flag arm repeater
    D. back light

20. With the track circuit unoccupied, the voltage at the relay end of the track circuit will be

    A. higher at the relay terminals than at the rails
    B. exactly half the feed-end voltage
    C. lower than the voltage at the track transformer
    D. the same as the feed-end voltage

21. If a test lamp lights when it is placed in series with a d.c. supply and a capacitor, the capacitor is *probably*

    A. bpen
    B. fully discharged
    C. shorted
    D. fully charged

22. The amount of leakage current in a track circuit depends LEAST on the

    A. type of track construction
    B. extent of wear of the running rails
    C. condition of the ballast
    D. length of the track circuit

23. One condition NOT likely to cause a track relay to be sluggish in picking up is a

    A. faulty insulated joint
    B. broken stop arm
    C. low feed end voltage
    D. Wet roadbed

24. G.T. signals are generally used when it is desired to

    A. limit the speed of trains through an interlocking
    B. limit the speed of trains on a long downgrade
    C. reduce speed of trains on upgrade
    D. allow trains to "close-in" in approach to an occupied station

QUESTIONS 25-29.

Questions 25-29 are based on the system of signal indications referred to in the paragraph below. Refer to this paragraph when answering these questions.

The entire transit system, except for a few instances, utilizes a system of interlocking signal indications that requires a train to come to a full stop before passing a home signal having a red aspect.

25. The signal aspect which means proceed with caution on diverging route prepare to stop at next signal is

    A. green over green
    B. yellow over green
    C. yellow over yellow
    D. green over green

26. The signal aspect which means proceed with caution on main route prepare to stop at next signal is

    A. green over yellow
    B. yellow over green
    C. yellow over yellow
    D. green over green

27. The signal aspect for a call-on is

    A. red over red over yellow
    B. yellow over yellow over yellow
    C. red over red over green
    D. yellow over yellow over green

28. The signal aspect which means proceed on diverging route is

    A. green over yellow
    B. yellow over yellow
    C. yellow over green
    D. green over green

29. The signal aspect which means proceed on main route is

    A. green over yellow
    B. yellow over yellow
    C. yellow over green
    D. green over green

30. One inspection item NOT made monthly on an alkaline storage battery is

    A. cell voltage of at least six cells
    B. specific gravity of electrolyte
    C. condition of terminals and terminal nuts
    D. condition of filler valve body

QUESTIONS 31-40.

Questions 31-40 are based on generally accepted transit system nomenclature.

31. The nomenclature for the normal switch correspondence relay is

    A. NWR   B. NWC   C. NWP   D. NWZ

32. The nomenclature HY stands for

    A. home caution relay
    B. home relay (slotting)
    C. home signal relay
    D. home yard relay

33. The letters used as a prefix for positive a.c. energy are
    A. BX   B. BH   C. LB   D. VB

34. The nomenclature for the distant control relay is
    A. DV   B. H   C. HS   D. COS

35. The nomenclature for the 14 volt. d.c. line battery is
    A. LS   B. H   C. LE   D. LB

36. The nomenclature for the home relay in a d.c. line control circuit is
    A. KR   B. H   C. COS   D. D

37. The nomenclature for the call-on relay is
    A. COS   B. C   C. CT   D. CGD

38. The nomenclature for the train stop is
    A. T   B. S   C. TS   D. V

39. The nomenclature for a time element relay is
    A. U   B. T   C. S   D. Q

40. The nomenclature for a track repeater relay is
    A. T   B. TP   C. TT   D. TR

KEY (CORRECT ANSWERS)

1. A	11. B	21. C	31. B
2. C	12. B	22. B	32. B
3. D	13. B	23. B	33. A
4. D	14. C	24. B	34. A
5. B	15. A	25. C	35. D
6. B	16. D	26. B	36. B
7. B	17. B	27. A	37. A
8. A	18. C	28. A	38. D
9. C	19. D	29. D	39. A
10. D	20. C	30. B	40. B

TEST 2

DIRECTIONS: Each question or incomplete statement is followed by several suggested answers or completions. Select the one that BEST answers the question or completes the statement. *PRINT THE LETTER OF THE CORRECT ANSWER IN THE SPACE AT THE RIGHT.*

QUESTIONS 1-10.

Questions 1 to 10 are concerned with territory where a.c. line controls are used. Refer to figure #1, in the sketch below when answering these questions.

The sketch below shows standard one-block-overlap control lines for automatic block signals as used by the transit system. That is, each signal remains red while either of the two track circuits in advance is occupied, and each signal changes to green when the signal in advance becomes yellow.

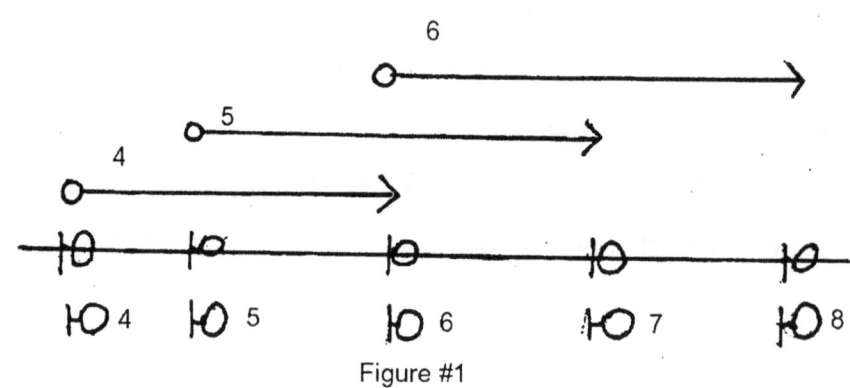
Figure #1

1. Signal #4 will be *red* if it is receiving energy through the

   A. front contact of 4HS relay
   B. back contact of 4HS relay
   C. front contact of 4D relay
   D. back contact of 4D relay

1.____

2. Signal #4 will be *yellow* if it is receiving energy through the

   A. front contact of 4HS relay
   B. back contact of 4HS relay
   C. front contact of 4D relay
   D. back contact of 4D relay

2.____

3. Signal #4 will be *green* if it is receiving energy through the

   A. front contact of 4HS relay
   B. back contact of 4HS relay
   C. front contact of 4D relay
   D. back contact of 4D relay

3.____

4. The control circuit for 4HS relay includes 4.____

   A. back contacts of 4T and 5T relay
   B. front contacts of 4T and 5T relay
   C. back contacts of 4D and 5D relay
   D. front contacts of 4D and 5D relay

5. The control circuit for the HS relay includes a stop contact to check that the stop 5.____

   A. is tripping after each train passes
   B. is clear for the next train
   C. arm is not broken
   D. has received energy

6. In order to insure that the next signal is not red the control circuit for 4D relay receives energy through a 6.____

   A. front contact in 4HS relay
   B. back contact in 4HS relay
   C. front contact in 5HS relay
   D. back contact in 5HS relay

7. Energy for this retaining control for the automatic stop associated with signal #4 is taken through a 7.____

   A. back contact in 4T relay
   B. front contact in 4T relay
   C. back contact in 4D relay
   D. front contact in 4D relay

8. A contact in the control circuit for 4D relay has the nomenclature 8.____

   A. 4VJ   B. 4T   C. 5T   D. 5V

9. The stick circuit feature on the HS relay is *necessary* 9.____

   A. to insure that the HS relay will pick up properly
   B. to insure that the stop arm is clear
   C. to hold the HS relay picked up
   D. since it is not of the biased neutral type

10. Energy for the control of all-electric stop mechanism is 10.____

    A. LB   B. BX   C. TB   D. BH

QUESTIONS 11-20.

Questions 11-20 are concerned with territory where d.c. line controls are used. Refer again to figure #1 when answering these questions.

11. Signal #4 will be *red* if it is receiving energy through the 11.____

    A. front contact of 4DV relay
    B. back contact of 4DV relay
    C. front contact of 4HV relay
    D. back contact of 4HV relay

12. Signal #4 will be *yellow* if it is receiving energy through the

   A. front contact of 4DV relay
   B. back contact of 4DV relay
   C. front contact of 4HV relay
   D. back contact of 4HV relay

12.____

13. Signal #4 will be *green* if it is receiving energy through the

   A. front contact of 4DV relay
   B. back contact of 4DV relay
   C. front contact of 4HV relay
   D. back contact of 4HV relay

13.____

14. The control circuit for 4HV relay includes a

   A. front contact of 4DV relay
   B. back contact of 4DV relay
   C. front contact of 4HV relay
   D. back contact of 4HV relay

14.____

15. In order to insure that the next signal is NOT red, the control circuit for 4DV relay receives energy through a

   A. front contact of 4T relay
   B. front contact of 5T relay
   C. front contact of 5HV relay
   D. back contact of 4H relay

15.____

16. The control circuit for 4HV relay includes a

   A. front contact of 4DV relay
   B. front contact of 4T relay
   C. front contact of 5T relay
   D. front contact of 4H relay

16.____

17. The control circuit for 4DV relay is fed with

   A. LB & BX energy
   B. BX & BH energy
   C. LB & VB energy
   D. BH & VB energy

17.____

18. The control circuit for 4HV relay includes a

   A. back contact of 4DV relay
   B. back contact of 4T relay
   C. stop contact
   D. back contact of 5T relay

18.____

19. If the distant relay for signal #4 is stuck in its de-energized position, the result will be that signal #4 will

   A. always display green
   B. never display yellow
   C. never display green
   D. be dark

19.____

20. Assume that signal #4 is green; signal #5 is yellow; and signal nos. 6, 7, and 8 are red. This condition would be brought about by a train on the track with its rear end

    A. between signals nos. 5 and 6
    B. between signals nos. 6 and 7
    C. between signals nos. 7 and 8
    D. past signal #8

21. Wire tags do NOT show the wire

    A. nomenclature
    B. location
    C. size
    D. destination

22. Safety considerations prohibit the use of carbon tetrachloride fire extinguishers on fires in the subway MAINLY because of the

    A. noxious fumes given off
    B. difficulty in refilling the extinguisher
    C. danger of damage to equipment
    D. shock hazard involved

23. The *normal* position of a switch lever on an all-electric conventional interlocking machine is

    A. pointing to the left
    B. pointing to the right
    C. pushed all the way in
    D. pulled all the way out

24. Standard flagging instructions require that the *minimum* distance a flagman is to place his portable trip and red lamp from the work area is

    A. 75 ft.
    B. 50 ft.
    C. two car lengths
    D. 1/2 car length

25. The emergency screw releases on an interlocking machine are proptected against unnecessary use by

    A. an alarm that cannot be silenced
    B. the control being in the trainmaster's office
    C. a lead seal
    D. a lock, with only the signal maintainer having a key

26. The distance from the gauge of rail to the side of the stop arm head nearest to the adjacent running rail is *approximately*

    A. 4"
    B. 5"
    C. 6"
    D. 7"

27. If a switch machine must be disconnected from the switch points, the FIRST person to be informed is the

    A. dispatcher
    B. supervisor, signals
    C. trainmaster
    D. towerman

28. One term that can *properly* be applied to the mechanical locking of a unit lever interlocking machine is

    A. apron
    B. bootleg
    C. dog
    D. frog

29. In accordance with standard practice on the transit system signal levers should be painted

    A. black   B. white   C. yellow   D. red

30. In accordance with standard practice on the transit system switch levers should be painted

    A. yellow   B. red   C. black   D. white

31. In accordance with standard practice on the transit system spare levers should be painted

    A. yellow   B. black   C. red   D. white

32. One color of light NOT used to convey information at the latest type of push button interlocking control panel is

    A. yellow   B. white   C. red   D. blue

33. A 10 to 1 step down transformer has an input of 2 amperes at 110 volts. If losses are neglected, the *maximum* output of the transformer is

    A. 2 amperes at 11 volts
    B. 20 amperes at 11 volts
    C. .2 amperes at 110 volts
    D. 20 amperes at 110 volts

34. A signal maintainer need NOT inform his relief that

    A. the relief signal foreman is on duty
    B. the telephone is out of order
    C. single track operation is in effect
    D. the track section is renewing rails

35. One advantage of the double rail track circuit as compared to the single rail track circuit is that the double rail track circuit

    A. heeds fewer insulated joints
    B. operates at a much lower current drain
    C. requires less equipment
    D. can be used for greater lengths of track circuits

36. The proper lantern signal to give a motorman to proceed past an out-of-service automatic signal in the subway is waving a

    A. white lantern across the track
    B. white lantern up and down
    C. green lantern across the track
    D. red lantern up and down

37. S.T. signals are generally used when it is desired to

    A. allow trains to "close-in" in approach to an occupied station
    B. limit speed of trains on a long downgrade
    C. reduce speed of trains on curves
    D. limit speed of trains through an interlocking

38. A signal maintainer would use a megger to test   38.____

    A. rail resistance   B. track voltage
    C. track current   D. insulation resistance

39. When connecting a track drill to operate from the third rail power, the BEST practice is to   39.____

    A. connect to the negative rail then to the third rail
    B. connect to the third rail then to the negative rail
    C. connect to the third rail and negative rail at the same time
    D. connect to the signal rail then to the third rail

40. Whenever it is necessary to sectionalize a high tension signal main, a signal maintainer MUST   40.____

    A. de-energize both feeders at the same time
    B. first notify the trainmaster
    C. do exactly as instructed by supervision
    D. de-energize normal power before cutting-in reverse power

KEY (CORRECT ANSWERS)

1. B	11. D	21. C	31. A
2. D	12. B	22. A	32. D
3. C	13. A	23. C	33. B
4. B	14. A	24. A	34. A
5. A	15. C	25. C	35. D
6. C	16. D	26. B	36. B
7. A	17. C	27. B	37. A
8. D	18. C	28. C	38. D
9. C	19. C	29. D	39. A
10. B	20. C	30. C	40. C

EXAMINATION SECTION
TEST 1

DIRECTIONS: Each question or incomplete statement is followed by several suggested answers or completions. Select the one that BEST answers the question or completes the statement. *PRINT THE LETTER OF THE CORRECT ANSWER IN THE SPACE AT THE RIGHT.*

1. In an air compressor plant, a signal maintainer would generally expect to find *two* 1.____

    A. compressor governors
    B. after-coolers
    C. manifold condensers
    D. air storage tanks

2. When a new switch is installed, the throw of the switch machine MUST be adjusted to the throw of the switch. This adjustment is provided for by 2.____

    A. a turnbuckle on the lock rod
    B. bolts on the switch rods
    C. set screws on the piston rod
    D. nuts on the throw rod

3. An IMPORTANT reason for shutting off the air *before* cranking or barring a switch to its opposite position is that the 3.____

    A. switch machine cylinder will be subjected to excessive pressure if air is left on
    B. switch will tend to restore if cranked out of agreement with its lever
    C. throw bar may become jammed on the operating cam
    D. stroke of the switch lever cannot be completed if air is not cut off

4. According to official instructions, the throw bar on a switch machine should be lubricated with 4.____

    A. light grease monthly
    B. medium oil monthly
    C. light grease weekly
    D. medium oil weekly

5. The MOST important reason that the emergency release must NOT be used if a train is approaching a switch, is that this would 5.____

    A. result in tripping the train
    B. make it possible to operate the switch under the train
    C. release the mechanical locking on conflicting signals
    D. be a violation of signal maintainers' instructions

6. Blow-off cocks are provided at various points on the compressed air system to 6.____

    A. blow dirt off exposed signal equipment
    B. reduce air line pressure to operating pressure at equipment locations
    C. vent accumulated condensation from the system
    D. protect compressor and storage tanks against excessive air pressure

7. A slow leak in an air line is MOST accurately located by

    A. moving a lighted match around the pipe near the leak
    B. holding the wet finger near the suspected leak
    C. listening closely for escaping air
    D. painting the suspected area with soap suds

8. The lever band over which the reverse magnet of a switch lever is energized to unlock the lever is designated by the symbol

    A. (RB)   B. (RD)   C. (RY)   D. (R)

9. At certain times, alcohol is fed into the air line in order to

    A. prevent the lubricant in air cylinders from becoming stiff
    B. keep the temperature of the air line from rising too high
    C. keep the temperature of the air line from falling too low
    D. keep condensed moisture from freezing in the equipment

10. Motion is transmitted from interlocking machine levers to the mechanical locking by means of

    A. cam slots and followers   B. links and cranks
    C. bevel gear sectors   D. racks and pinions

11. Motion is transmitted from interlocking machine levers to the vertical shafts carrying the band contacts by means of

    A. cam slots and followers   B. links and cranks
    C. bevel gear sectors   D. racks and pinions

12. A towerman reports that the model board indication for a certain yard track section including a switch is "occupied," while he can see out of the tower window that the track section is clear.
    A *possible* cuase of this condition is a short circuited

    A. normal lever band on the switch lever
    B. track fuse
    C. back contact on the track relay
    D. lock valve magnet

13. Branches from the main air line in the subway are taken from the top of the pipe. This practice is followed to

    A. take advantage of the natural upward flow of air
    B. insure adequate clearance for anyone walking on the bench walk
    C. facilitate carrying the branch line over the roof of the subway to the operating unit
    D. minimize the amount of moisture carried to equipment

14. In *most* compressor plants, the total number of valves that MUST be either opened or closed to by-pass an after-cooler that is to be repaired is

    A. 5   B. 4   C. 3   D. 2

15. If the point of a switch separates from the stock rail by *more* than a predetermined amount, the switch machine acts to restore the point tightly against the stock rail. The restoring action is started by the opening of contacts in the

    A. detector track relay
    B. switch circuit controler
    C. interlocking machine
    D. switch valve

16. An *appropriate* size designation for a tee to be used in taking a tap off the main air line is

    A. 2" x 2" x 1/2"   B. 1 1/2" x 1" x 1 1/2"
    C. 1" x 2 1/2" x 2 1/2" D. 2 1/2" x 1/x 2"

17. A signal lever band which positively indicates that the lever on which it is used controls two opposing signals is

    A. (LD)   B. (ND)   C. (DE)   D. (RD)

18. A certain switch lever is readily moved out of the reverse position but CANNOT be moved past mid-stroke.
    The fault is *most likely* that

    A. an open has occured in the latch circuit
    B. the latch has jammed in the quadrant
    C. a piece of cross locking has broken
    D. there is a cross in the indication circuit

19. If the lever in the preceding question can be moved past mid-stroke as far as the normal indication position, but the stroke CANNOT be completed to the full normal position, the fault is LEAST likely to be that

    A. there is an obstruction in the switch point
    B. an open has developed in the normal indication circuit
    C. the switch heels are too tight
    D. the lever shaft bearings are binding

20. A maintainer could quickly eliminate "open detector circuit" as the fault in question 18 by the fact that the

    A. detector light remained dark
    B. switch remained in its reverse position
    C. lever was free to move
    D. indication was not received

21. On finding a signal lever which could NOT be moved from its extreme right position, you could *correctly* conclude that

    A. a part of the mechanical locking had jammed
    B. the signal had not responded to the lever movement
    C. there was a train passing the signal
    D. an interlocked switch lever has been left at mid-stroke

22. The result of excessive wear of the quadrant or latch on a switch lever will be that the

    A. indication magnets will overheat due to being energized continuously
    B. switch will start in motion before the lever reaches the operating position
    C. lever segments will jam against the magnet latches
    D. stroke of the lever can be completed before receipt of an indication

23. Resistors having a value of 130-ohms each are used in the magnet valve control circuits of some switch machines. These resistors are used when the

    A. switch is operated frequently and the valve magnets may overheat
    B. switch lever controls only a single switch
    C. switch machine has low resistance magnet valves
    D. supply voltage is too high for normal operation

24. The two pistons of a type CP switch valve are mechanically interconnected by a walking beam.
    The purpose of the walking beam is to

    A. provide a simple means of moving the valve pistons for maintenance purposes
    B. permit the use of light springs in the poppet valves
    C. make the indicating contacts fast-acting
    D. prevent the admission of air to both switch machine cylinders simultaneously

25. Normal position of a signal lever *generally* is

    A. down and to the left   B. up and to the right
    C. straight down   D. straight up

26. Reverse position of a switch lever *generally* is

    A. down and to the left   B. up and to the right
    C. straight down   D. straight up

27. In air compressor plants, the governors are set to start the first motor when the air pressure falls to a prescribed minimum.
    The number *nearest* to the prescribed minimum pounds per square inch is

    A. 57   B. 63   C. 70   D. 73

28. The fact that when lever No. 3 is reversed, it locks lever No. 5 in its reverse position, and lever No. 8 in its normal position, could be briefly written as

    A. 3R Locks 5 ⑧   B. 3 Locks 5 ⑧
    C. 3 R Locks ⑤ 8   D. 3 Locks ⑤ 8

29. Energizing a valve magnet moves the pin valve so as to

    A. *close* the port to atmosphere and open the port to the air supply
    B. *open* the port to atmosphere and close the port to the air supply
    C. *close* both the port to atmosphere and the port to the air supply
    D. *open* both the port to atmosphere and the port to the air supply

30. Before doing any work the nature of which might cause a signal to display a false clear indication, the maintainer MUST make sure that the signal displays the stop indication and that it CANNOT clear until the work is completed.
    A job which would come under this rule is

    A. checking the operation of mechanical time releases
    B. changing out a plug-in type home relay
    C. replacing a burned out track resistor
    D. adjusting switch circuit controller contacts

31. The letters "SS" on IRT wiring diagrams or the letters "KR" on IND wiring diagrams designate a

    A. switch indication relay   B. switch detector relay
    C. stop repeater relay   D. dwarf signal relay

32. The circuit which is made by pressing the push button associated with a signal lever is the

    A. home control   B. route locking
    C. call-on control   D. switch operating

33. According to official instructions, the outboard bearing of a train stop should be lubricated with

    A. light grease monthly   B. light grease weekly
    C. medium oil monthly   D. medium oil weekly

34. The symbol on a signal circuit drawing which represents a lever band closing the circuit from the reverse position to the normal indication position is a circle around the letters

    A. RB   B. RC   C. RD   D. RY

35. The symbol on a signal circuit drawing which represents a lever band closing the circuit from the normal position to the reverse indication position is a circle around the letters

    A. NX   B. ND   C. NC   D. NB

36. If the click of the indication magnet is heard when the latch on a switch lever is turned, it indicates the

    A. home signal is normal
    B. controlled switch is clear of trains
    C. lever is free to move
    D. indicating circuit is clear of grounds

37. Complete stroke of a switch lever from full normal to full reverse is _____ degrees.

    A. 30   B. 60   C. 90   D. 120

38. To be sure the compressor starts with NO load, an un-loader is included with each compressor used on the signal system.
    Unloader functions by

    A. keeping the intake valve closed   B. keeping the exhaust valve closed
    C. holding the intake valve open   D. holding the exhaust valve open

39. D.C. control voltage used on interlocking machines is about

 A. 32 volts   B. 24 volts   C. 12 volts   D. 10 volts

40. Designation 3WC on the IRT Division or 3WS on the other divisions refers to a

 A. stop relay
 B. magnet valve
 C. switch lever lock
 D. route locking relay

KEY (CORRECT ANSWERS)

1. A	11. C	21. A	31. A
2. D	12. C	22. C	32. C
3. B	13. D	23. B	33. A
4. B	14. C	24. D	34. A
5. B	15. B	25. C	35. B
6. C	16. A	26. B	36. B
7. D	17. A	27. B	37. B
8. C	18. D	28. D	38. C
9. D	19. D	29. A	39. B
10. D	20. C	30. D	40. D

TEST 2

DIRECTIONS: Each question or incomplete statement is followed by several suggested answers or completions. Select the one that BEST answers the question or completes the statement. *PRINT THE LETTER OF THE CORRECT ANSWER IN THE SPACE AT THE RIGHT.*

1. The pressure of contact fingers in switch machines MUST be maintained within specified limits to insure proper operation.
   The pressure of such contact fingers is measured by means of a

   A. pressure gauge
   B. spring scale
   C. torsion balance
   D. strain gauge

2. *Before* disconnecting a switch machine from a track switch, it is NOT necessary for the maintainer to

   A. remove power from the third rail
   B. see that the switch is clamped or spiked in position
   C. see that all signals protecting the switch are displaying their stop indications
   D. notify the towerman

3. Mechanical locking is made to operate easily and smoothly by the use of

   A. graphite lubricant
   B. light oil or grease
   C. lard lubricant
   D. powdered soapstone

4. One indication of failure of switch rod insulation would be

   A. energizing of the lock magnet
   B. locking of associated signal levers
   C. blowing of the track feed fuse
   D. darkening of the detector light

5. A lever band which positively indicates that the lever on which it is used controls two opposing signals is

   A. - (LB)   B. - (AB)   C. - (BN)   D. - (RB)

6. A lever time release is *generally* used to shunt out contacts on the

   A. lever latch
   B. approaching track relay
   C. detector relay
   D. lever magnet

7. A towerman tells you that he CANNOT move a particular switch lever although he can see that the track is clear. You will have a positive clue to the possible cause of trouble if you find that the

   A. air pressure gauge reads 70 pounds
   B. levers of all interlocked signals are normal
   C. switch is laying in the reverse position
   D. model board indicates the switch section to be occupied

8. A certain switch lever is readily moved out of the normal position but CANNOT be moved past mid-stroke.
   The fault is *most* likely that

   A. the latch has jammed in the quadrant
   B. a piece of cross locking has broken
   C. there is a cross in the indication circuit
   D. an open has occurred in the latch circuit

9. If the lever in the preceding question can be moved past mid-stroke as far as the reverse indication position, but the stroke cannot be completed to the full reverse position, the fault is LEAST likely to be that

   A. the switch heels are too tight
   B. the lever shaft bearings are binding
   C. there is an obstruction in the switch point
   D. an open has developed in the reverse indication circuit

10. A maintainer could quickly eliminate "open detector circuit" as the fault in question 8 by the fact that the

    A. lever was free to move
    B. indication was not received
    C. detector light remained dark
    D. switch remained in its normal position

11. On finding a signal lever which could NOT be moved from its extreme right position, you could correctly conclude that

    A. the signal had not responded to the lever movement
    B. an interlocked switch lever had been left at mid-stroke
    C. a part of the mechanical locking had jammed
    D. there was a train passing the signal

12. Maintainers are required to see that all signal relay cases are not only kept closed, but locked.
    Locking is required *primarily* to guard the equipment against

    A. theft   B. steel dust   C. moisture   D. tampering

13. Blow-off cocks are provided at various points on the compressed air system to

    A. reduce air line pressure to operating pressure at equipment locations
    B. blow dirt off exposed signal equipment
    C. protect compressor and storage tanks against excessive air pressure
    D. vent accumulated condensation from the system

14. A slow leak in an air line is most accurately located by

    A. holding the wet finger near the suspected leak
    B. listening closely for escaping air
    C. painting the suspected area with soap suds
    D. moving a lighted match around the pipe near the leak

15. The amount of throw of a track switch is *closest* to

    A. 6 inches   B. 5 1/2 inches   C. 3 1/2 inches   D. inches

16. The air supply to a certain switch machine is cut off and the switch is cranked fully over to the other position.
    If the air supply is now restored, the result will be that the

    A. switch valves will be blocked in the new position
    B. switch lever will not correspond in position with the switch
    C. switch will return to its original position
    D. signals controlling movements over the switch will be locked out

17. Branches from the main air line in the subway are taken from the top of the pipe.
    This practice is followed to

    A. minimize the amount of moisture carried to equipment
    B. facilitate carrying the branch line over the roof of the subway to the operating unit
    C. insure adequate clearance for anyone walking on the bench walk
    D. take advantage of the natural upward flow of air

18. Standard practice on the transit system is to paint switch levers

    A. blue   B. black   C. red   D. white

19. Signal levers on the transit system are painted

    A. blue   B. black   C. red   D. white

20. If both of the compressors at an average interlocking plant are out of service, the plant can be operated *normally* from the interlocking machine

    A. less than an hour   B. 6 to 8 hours
    C. about one day   D. indefinitely

21. In most compressor plants, the total number of valves that must be either opened or closed to by-pass a manifold condenser that is to be repaired is

    A. 2   B. 3   C. 4   D. 5

22. If the point of a switch separates from the stock rail by more than a predetermined amount, the switch machine acts to restore the point tightly against the stock rail.
    This restoring action is started by the opening of contacts in the

    A. switch circuit controller   B. interlocking machine
    C. switch valve   D. detector track relay

23. Of the following, noisy chattering of a track relay is *most likely* due to a

    A. stiff spring on a front contact
    B. high voltage on the local winding
    C. loose connection in a track lead
    D. broken signal-rail bond

24. An *appropriate* size designation for a tee to be used in taking a tap off the main air line is

    A. 1/2" x 2" x 3" B. 1" x 2" x 3"
    C. 3" x 1" x 3"   D. 2" x 2" x 1/2"

25. The distance between the center line of the automatic stop arm and the gauge of the running rail is *nearest* to

    A. 2 1/2 inches   B. 5 inches   C. 7 inches   D. 8 1inches

QUESTIONS 26-29.

Questions 26-29 inclusive in Column I are symbols for various contact bands used on switch levers, each of which represents one of the contact bands shown in Column II. For each symbol in Column I, select the appropriate contact band from Column II. PRINT on your answer sheet, in the correspondingly numbered item space, the letter given beside your selected band.

Column I   Column II
(symbols)   (contact bands)

26.

    A.

27.

    B.

28.

    C.

29.

    D.

30. The function of the safety tooth on a switch lever segment is to

    A. prevent completion of the lever stroke if there is a cross
    B. insure proper starting of the mechanical time release
    C. prevent overtravel of the mechanical cross locking
    D. insure proper contact with the latch depressor

31. To be sure that the compressor starts with NO load, an unloader is included with each compressor used on the signal system.
The unloader functions by

   A. keeping the exhaust valve closed
   B. holding the exhaust valve open
   C. keeping the intake valve closed
   D. holding the intake valve open

31.____

32. If the click of the indication magnet is heard when the latch on a switch lever is turned, it is an indication that the

   A. lever is free to move
   B. home signal is clear
   C. indicating circuit is clear of grounds
   D. controlled switch is clear of trains

32.____

33. The result of *excessive* wear of the quadrant or latch on a switch lever will be that the

   A. stroke of the lever can be completed before receipt of an indication
   B. indication magnets will overheat due to being energized continuously
   C. switch will start its motion before the lever reaches the operating position
   D. lever segments will jam against the magnet latches

33.____

34. Resistors having a value of 130-ohms each are used in the control circuits of some switch machines.
These resistors are used when the

   A. switch lever controls only a single switch
   B. switch machine has low resistance magnet valves
   C. supply voltage is too high for normal operation
   D. switch is operated frequently and the valve magnets may overheat

34.____

35. Energizing a valve magnet moves the pin valve so as to

   A. *close* both the port to atmosphere and the air supply
   B. *open* both the port to atmosphere and the air supply
   C. *close* the port to atmosphere and open the air supply
   D. *open* the port to atmosphere and close off the air supply

35.____

36. The lever band over which the normal magnet of a switch lever is energized to *unlock* the lever is designated by the symbol

   A. -(N)   B. -(NX)   C. -(NB)   D. -(ND)

36.____

37. Alcohol is fed into the air lines in cold weather to

   A. dissolve accumulated grease, thus preventing clogging
   B. keep condensed moisture from freezing in the equipment
   C. prevent the lubricant in air cylinders from becoming stiff
   D. cool the air to the outside temperature

37.____

38. Motion is transmitted from interlocking machine levers to the mechanical locking by means of

    A. racks and pinions
    B. bevel gear sectors
    C. links and cranks
    D. cam slots and followers

39. Motion is transmitted from interlocking machine levers to the vertical shafts carrying the band contacts by means of

    A. racks and pinions
    B. bevel gear sectors
    C. links and cranks
    D. cam slots and followers

40. *Before* attempting to crank a switch, a maintainer must ALWAYS

    A. shut off the air
    B. cut off third rail power
    C. notify the nearest dispatcher
    D. notify his foreman

KEY (CORRECT ANSWERS)

1. B	11. C	21. B	31. D
2. A	12. D	22. A	32. D
3. B	13. D	23. C	33. D
4. D	14. C	24. D	34. A
5. D	15. C	25. C	35. C
6. B	16. C	26. D	36. B
7. D	17. A	27. C	37. B
8. B	18. B	28. B	38. A
9. C	19. C	29. A	39. B
10. A	20. D	30. A	40. A

EXAMINATION SECTION
TEST 1

DIRECTIONS: Each question or incomplete statement is followed by several suggested answers or completions. Select the one that BEST answers the question or completes the statement. *PRINT THE LETTER OF THE CORRECT ANSWER IN THE SPACE AT THE RIGHT.*

1. The *proper* way to clean the commutator of a switch machine motor is to use 1.____

    A. steel wool
    B. emery cloth
    C. cloth rubbed with vaseline
    D. chamois moistened with oil

2. The track relay used in conjunction with a balancing reactor has 2.____

    A. oversize control terminals
    B. a return spring instead of a counterweight
    C. two equal track windings
    D. a vane-type rotor

3. Safety magnets in interlocking machines are connected in the _____ circuits. 3.____

    A. signal operating
    B. switch indication
    C. switch operating
    D. signal indication

4. The PRINCIPAL purpose of the electro-magnetic brake on a switch machine is to 4.____

    A. stop the motor when the indication has been completed
    B. prevent the motor from turning when there is a cross
    C. prevent jarring open of the switch under a train if the mechanism becomes unlocked
    D. avoid slamming the switch point against the stock rail

5. The *standard* way of determining the state of charge of an Edison storage battery in interlocking plant service is to measure the 5.____

    A. level of the electrolyte
    B. specific gravity of the electrolyte
    C. amperage of each cell
    D. voltage of each cell

6. According to official instructions, the outboard bearing of a train stop should be lubricated with 6.____

    A. light grease monthly
    B. light grease weekly
    C. medium oil monthly
    D. medium oil weekly

7. Before doing any work the nature of which might cause a signal to display a false clear indication, the maintainer must make sure that the signal displays the stop indication and that it CANNOT clear until the work it completed. 7.____
A job which would come under this rule is

    A. changing out a plug-in type home relay
    B. replacing a burned out track resistor

109

C. adjusting switch circuit controller contacts
D. checking the operation of polar relays

8. The fact that when lever No. 2 is reversed it locks lever No. 5 in its reverse position and lever No. 8 in its normal position could be briefly written as

   A. 2 locks 5 ⑧
   B. 2 locks ⑤ 8
   C. ② locks ⑤ 8
   D. ② locks 5 ⑧

9. A signal maintainer notices that a stop which operated properly before is now sluggish when clearing. To correct this fault it would be *good* procedure to FIRST

   A. check the outboard bearing for binding and lubrication
   B. increase the voltage at the stop motor
   C. check the resistance of the hold-clear contacts in the motor circuit
   D. inspect the stop motor circuit for loose connections

10. The circuit which is completed by the energizing of the WR relay is the _____ circuit.

    A. switch operating
    B. signal indication
    C. stop clearing
    D. traffic lock

11. The *usual* number of Edison storage cells at an interlocking plant is

    A. 60
    B. 90
    C. 110
    D. 120

12. Motion is transmitted from interlocking machine levers to the mechanical locking by means of

    A. cam slots and followers
    B. links and cranks
    C. bevel gear sectors
    D. racks and pinions

13. Motion is transmitted from interlocking machine levers to the vertical shafts carrying the band contacts by means of

    A. cam slots and followers
    B. links and cranks
    C. bevel gear sectors
    D. racks and pinions

14. An IMPORTANT reason for cutting out the switch machine motor before cranking over a switch is that the

    A. dynamic indication will be lost if power is left on
    B. brake cannot be released if power is left on
    C. clutch will be damaged if cranked in the opposite direction from the motor
    D. switch will tend to restore if cranked out of agreement with its lever

15. When a new switch is installed, the throw of the switch machine must be adjusted to the throw of the switch. This adjustment is provided for by   15.____

    A. nuts on the throw rod
    B. a slot in the cam bar
    C. a turnbuckle on the lock rod
    D. nuts on the driving clutch

16. When a signal lever is moved from the reverse position to the normal position, the indication of the controlled signal should change from "proceed" to "stop"   16.____

    A. when the lever reaches the indication position
    B. as the lever leaves the reverse position
    C. after the lever time release has operated
    D. when the lever reaches mid-stroke

17. The fault that would cause one of the polar relays in the cabinet at the end of the interlocking machine to open is   17.____

    A. crossed signal control wires
    B. grounded switch control wires
    C. failure of a signal to clear
    D. excessive switch operating current

18. The polar relay in the preceding question is *normally* held closed by the   18.____

    A. lever latch   B. permanent magnet
    C. indication current   D. mechanical locking

19. The lever controlling a crossover is moved from the full reverse to the normal indication position. The ammeter needle swings to 14 amperes then to 10 amperes where it remains a few seconds and then falls to zero.
These ammeter readings indicate that   19.____

    A. both switches have operated normally
    B. a switch operating fuse has blown
    C. a switch part is binding at the start of the movement
    D. there is an obstruction in the switch point

20. The lever controlling a crossover is moved from full normal to the reverse indication position. The ammeter needle swings up to 7 amperes, drops almost immediately to 5 amperes where it remains for a few seconds, and then falls to zero.
These ammeter readings indicate that   20.____

    A. both switches have operated normally
    B. a switch operating fuse has blown
    C. some part of the switch mechanism is binding at the beginning of the movement
    D. there is an obstruction in a switch point

21. The lever controlling a turnout is moved as in question 19. The ammeter needle swings up to 7 amperes, drops almost immediately to 5 amperes where it remains for a few seconds, then rises to 8 amperes and remains there. This action of the ammeter could NOT be due to   21.____

A. tight switch heels
B. the throw of the switch machine having come out of adjustment
C. binding of the operating lever
D. an obstruction in the switch point

22. When the lever controlling a turnout is moved as in question 20, the ammeter reading becomes, and remains, a half-ampere.
This is an indication that the

A. polar relay has opened
B. switch motor circuit is open
C. indication magnets are short circuited
D. pole changer is short circuited

23. A switch lever controlling a turnout is moved as in question 19, and the ammeter continues to read zero. The fault is *most likely* to be that

A. a brush has broken in the switch machine motor
B. pole changer is mechanically jammed
C. there is an open in the indication circuit
D. an open has developed in the normal control wire

24. A maintainer could quickly eliminate "open detector circuit" as the fault in the preceding question by the fact that the

A. polar relay remained closed
B. lever was free to move
C. detector light remained dark
D. indication was not received

25. A switch repeater relay would be indicated on the signal wiring diagrams by the letters

A. NW   B. RW   C. WR   D. WP

26. In normal operation, after the movement of a track switch has been completed and power has been cut off, the motor of the switch machine makes several additional revolutions. The reason for these extra revolutions is to

A. unlock the pole changer
B. lock the switch up tight against the stock rail
C. generate current to energize the indication magnet
D. generate current to energize the indication selector

27. If the indication selector fails to operate when a switch lever is moved from normal toward reverse, the result will be that the

A. detector light will remain dark
B. switch operating fuse will blow out
C. indication magnet will become hot and may burn out
D. lever cannot be moved past reverse indication position

28. When a switch lever is moved from the reverse position to the normal indication position, the FIRST item of equipment to complete its movement is the

    A. motor
    B. pole changer
    C. indication selector
    D. indication magnet

29. According to official instructions, the throw bar on a switch machine should be lubricated with

    A. light grease monthly
    B. light grease weekly
    C. medium oil monthly
    D. medium oil weekly

30. The MOST important reason that the emergency release must NOT be used if a train is approaching a switch, is that this would

    A. be a violation of signal maintainers' instructions
    B. result in tripping the train
    C. make it possible to operate the switch under the train
    D. release the mechanical locking on conflicting signals

31. If the click of the lever lock is heard when the latch on a switch lever is squeezed, it is an indication that the

    A. home signal is clear
    B. indication circuit is clear of grounds
    C. controlled switch is clear of trains
    D. lever is free to move

32. The symbol on a signal circuit drawing which represents a lever band closing the circuit from the reverse position to the normal indication position is a circle around the letters

    A. RY   B. RD   C. RC   D. RB

33. The symbol on a signal circuit drawing which represents a lever band closing the circuit from the normal position to the reverse indication position is a circle around the letters

    A. NB   B. NC   C. ND   D. NX

34. The adjustment of contacts operated by a switch circuit controller should be checked by

    A. operating the switch lever
    B. operating the affected signal levers
    C. cranking the switch
    D. using feeler gages

35. An accumulation of hard salts blocking the valve in the filler cap of an Edison storage cell *might* result in

    A. bulging of the case
    B. limiting the charge to less than a full charge
    C. buckling of the plates
    D. corrosion of the terminals

36. The BEST immediate first aid if electrolyte splashes in the eyes when filling a storage battery is to

   A. bandage the eyes to keep out the light
   B. induce tears to flow by staring at a bright light
   C. wipe the eyes dry with a soft cloth
   D. bathe the eyes with plenty of clean water

37. The MOST serious consequence of excessive contact pressure in the pole changer assembly is the tendency to

   A. hold the pole changer inoperative when required to operate electrically
   B. buckle the stationary contacts each time the pole changer operates
   C. wear away the moving contact bars rapidly
   D. lose the dynamic indication

38. The complete stroke of a lever from full normal to full reverse is *nearest* to

   A. 2"   B. 3"   C. 4"   D. 5"

39. With respect to a throw bar, it could be *correct* to say that it is

   A. full stroke   B. left hand
   C. quick-acting   D. semi-automatic

40. The one of the following relays which is LEAST likely to have any of its contacts in the home control circuit of an interlocking home signal is a

   A. switch repeater
   B. switch detector and cut-off
   C. track repeater
   D. call-on

KEY (CORRECT ANSWERS)

1. D	11. B	21. C	31. C
2. C	12. A	22. B	32. D
3. C	13. B	23. D	33. C
4. C	14. D	24. B	34. C
5. D	15. A	25. D	35. A
6. A	16. B	26. C	36. D
7. C	17. B	27. D	37. A
8. B	18. B	28. C	38. B
9. A	19. A	29. C	39. B
10. A	20. B	30. C	40. B

TEST 2

DIRECTIONS: Each question or incomplete statement is followed by several suggested answers or completions. Select the one that BEST answers the question or completes the statement. *PRINT THE LETTER OF THE CORRECT ANSWER IN THE SPACE AT THE RIGHT.*

1. The pressure of contact fingers in switch machines must be maintained within specified limits to insure proper operation. The pressure of such contact fingers is measured by means of a

    A. torsion balance
    B. strain gauge
    C. spring scale
    D. pressure gauge

    1.____

2. *Before* disconnecting a switch machine from a track switch, it is NOT necessary for the maintainer to

    A. see that the switch is spiked or clamped in position
    B. notify the towerman
    C. remove power from the third rail
    D. see that all signals protecting the switch are displaying their stop indications

    2.____

3. Mechanical locking is made to operate easily and smoothly by the use of

    A. lard lubricant
    B. powdered soapstone
    C. graphite lubricant
    D. light oil or grease

    3.____

4. ONE indication of failure of switch rod insulation would be

    A. darkening of the detector light
    B. blowing of the track feed fuse
    C. locking of associated signal levers
    D. opening of the polar relay

    4.____

5. A switch lever band switch is used in the switch repeater relay circuit is

    A. — (WR)   B. — (NB)   C. — (ND)   D. — (BD)

    5.____

6. A lever time release is *generally* used to shunt out contacts on the

    A. detector relay
    B. WR relay
    C. lever magnet
    D. approach track relay

    6.____

7. A towerman tells you that he CANNOT move a particular switch lever although he can see that the track is clear. You will have a positive clue to the possible cause of the trouble if you find that the

    A. switch is lying in the reverse position
    B. model board indicates the switch section to be occupied
    C. levers of all interlocked signals are normal
    D. the switch operating fuse is blown

    7.____

8. The lever controlling a crossover is moved from full normal to the reverse indication position. The ammeter needle swings up to 7 amperes, drops almost immediately to 5 amperes where it remains for a few seconds, and then falls to zero. These ammeter readings indicate that

    A. a switch operating fuse has blown
    B. both switches have operated normally
    C. there is an obstruction in a switch point
    D. some part of the switch mechanism is binding at the beginning of the movement

9. The lever controlling a turnout is moved as in question 8.
    The ammeter needle swings up to 7 amperes, drops almost immediately to 5 amperes where it remains for a few seconds, then rises to 8 amperes and remains there.
    This action of the ammeter could NOT be due to

    A. an obstruction in the switch point
    B. tight switch heels
    C. the throw of the switch machine having come out of adjustment
    D. binding of the operating lever

10. When the lever controlling a turnout is moved as in question 8, the ammeter reading becomes and remains a half-ampere. This is an indication that the

    A. pole changer is short circuited
    B. indication magnets are short circuited
    C. switch motor circuit is open
    D. polar relay has opened

11. A switch lever controlling a turnout is moved as in question 8, and the ammeter continues to read zero.
    The fault is *most likely* to be that

    A. the switch operating fuse has blown
    B. a brush has broken in the switch machine motor
    C. an open has developed in the normal control wire
    D. there is an open in the indication circuit

12. A maintainer could quickly eliminate "open detector circuit" by the fact that the

    A. detector light remained dark
    B. polar relay remained closed
    C. lever was free to move
    D. indication was not received

13. The PRINCIPAL purpose of the balancing impedance used on many single-rail track circuits of the transit system is to

    A. *minimize* the effect of d.c. on the operation of the track relay
    B. *equalize* the signal current between the two track windings of the track relay
    C. *shunt* d.c. around the track windings of the track relay
    D. *boost* the track voltage to insure good pick-up

14. The *probable* result of shunting out the purely resistance portion of the balancing impedance in the preceding question would be   14.____

    A. weak pick-up of the track relay
    B. chattering of the track relay due to d.c.
    C. overheating of the track transformer
    D. increased track circuit leakage

15. The amount of throw of a track switch is closest to   15.____

    A. 5 1/2 inches   B. 6 inches   C. 2 inches   D. 3 inches

16. The LOWEST point to which the level of the electrolyte in Edison cells should be permitted to fall is   16.____

    A. 1/4 inch below the tops of the plates
    B. even with the tops of the plates
    C. 1/4 inch above the tops of the plates
    D. 1 1/4 inches above the tops of the plates

17. If the level of the electrolyte in several of the cells of an Edison battery is found to be considerably *below* the level in the remaining cells, the maintainer should inspect these cells for   17.____

    A. loose connections
    B. leaky containers
    C. short circuited terminals
    D. damaged plates

18. Standard practice on the transit system is to paint switch levers   18.____

    A. black   B. white   C. blue   D. red

19. Signal levers on the transit system are painted   19.____

    A. black   B. white   C. blue   D. red

20. The commutator of a switch machine motor is *preferably* cleaned by rubbing with   20.____

    A. steel wool   B. chamois skin
    C. cotton waste   D. emery cloth

21. The cut-out contact on a certain switch machine is opened and the switch is cranked fully over to the other position. If the cut-out is now *closed*, the result will be that   21.____

    A. the switch operating fuse will blow out
    B. the polar relay will open and sound an alarm
    C. the switch will return to its original position
    D. neither switch repeater relay will pick up

22. The careless act which is *most likely* to result in a personal injury is leaving   22.____

    A. a bench vise with its jaws not fully closed
    B. a hammer and files in the same bench drawer
    C. a tower relay cabinet door unlocked
    D. a drawer in a workbench half open

23. Of the following, noisy chattering of a track relay is *most likely* due to a

   A. high voltage on the local winding
   B. staff spring on a front contact
   C. broken signal-rail bond
   D. loose connection in a track lead

24. The circuit which is made by pressing the push button above a signal lever is

   A. call-on control
   B. route locking
   C. home control
   D. switch repeater

25. A circuit which is completed through contacts on the emergency release but which is broken at the start of emergency release operation is the

   A. call-on control
   B. route locking
   C. home control
   D. switch repeater

QUESTIONS 26-29.

Questions 26-29 inclusive in Column I are descriptions of various contact springs used on switch lever circuit controllers, each of which refers to one of the springs shown in Column II. For each description in Column I, select the appropriate spring from Column II. PRINT on your answer sheet, in the correspondingly numbered item space, the letter given beside your selected spring.

Column I
(descriptions)

Column II
(contact springs)

26. Closes circuit from center to full normal positions.

27. Closes circuit from normal to normal indication positions.

28. Closes circuit only at the normal indication position.

29. Closes circuit only at the full normal position.

30. The fault that would cause one of the polar relays in the cabinet at the end of the interlocking machine to open is

   A. excessive switch operating current
   B. failure of a signal to clear
   C. grounded switch control wires
   D. crossed signal control wires

31. The polar relay in the preceding question is normally held *closed* by the

     A. mechanical locking
     B. indication current
     C. permanent magnet
     D. lever latch

32. If the indication selector fails to operate when a lever is moved from normal toward reverse, the result will be that the

     A. lever CANNOT be moved past the reverse indication position
     B. indication magnet will become hot and may burn out
     C. switch operating fuse will blow out
     D. detector light will become dark

33. The circuit which is completed by the energizing of the WR relay is the _____ circuit.

     A. switch operating
     B. signal indication
     C. stop clearing
     D. traffic lock

34. When two or more signals are controlled by one lever, as home signals are frequently controlled in yards, the selection as to which signal will clear when the lever is reversed is generally made over the

     A. lever bands
     B. switch repeater relays or bands
     C. detector relays
     D. switch circuit contrlers

35. A maintainer connects one 110-volt lamp between the NW and CW wires, and another identical lamp between the RW and CW wires, in the back of the interlocking machine. If the switch lever is fully normal

     A. both lamps should be dark
     B. both lamps should be lighted
     C. the lamp connected to the RW wire should be lighted, while the other is dark
     D. the lamp connected to the NW wire should be lighted, while the other is dark

36. After the switch lever in the preceding question has been moved to the reverse operating position and the switch has operated

     A. both lamps should be dark
     B. both lamps should be lighted
     C. the lamp connected to the RW wire should be lighted, while the other is dark
     D. the lamp connected to the NW wire should be lighted, while the other is dark

37. When a home signal clears, the stop motor, home relay, and hold-clear coil are energized, but NOT in that order.
    The correct order (for the latest circuit in use) is

     A. home relay, stop motor, hold-clear coil
     B. stop motor, hold-clear coil, home relay
     C. home relay, hold-clear coil, stop motor
     D. hold-clear coil, home relay, stop motor

38. Motion is transmitted from interlocking machine levers to to the mechanical locking by means of

     A. racks and pinions
     B. bevel gear sectors
     C. links and cranks
     D. cam slots and followers

39. Motion is transmitted from interlocking machine levers to the vertical shafts carrying the band contacts by means of

    A. racks and pinions
    B. bevel gear selectors
    C. links and cranks
    D. cam slots and followers

40. Before attempting to crank a switch, a maintainer must ALWAYS

    A. cut off third rail power
    B. notify the nearest dispatcher
    C. notify his foreman
    D. cut off power to the switch

KEY (CORRECT ANSWERS)

1. C	11. A	21. C	31. C
2. C	12. C	22. D	32. A
3. D	13. A	23. D	33. A
4. A	14. B	24. A	34. B
5. B	15. D	25. D	35. D
6. D	16. D	26. C	36. C
7. B	17. B	27. A	37. C
8. A	18. A	28. D	38. D
9. D	19. D	29. B	39. C
10. C	20. B	30. C	40. D